WHERE DID GOD COME FROM?

The Eternal Nature and Sovereignty of God

Dr. Maxwell R. Shimba

Copyright © 2024 – Dr. Maxwell R. Shimba

All rights reserved. No portion of this book may be reproduced, stored in a retrieval system, or transmitted in any form or by any means – electronics, mechanical, photocopy, recording, scanning, or other – except for brief quotations in critical reviews or articles, without the prior written permission of the publisher.

Shimba Publishing, LLC.

Printed by Shimba Publishing LLC
Printed in the United States of America

TABLE OF CONTENTS

INTRODUCTION

Introduction: Exploring the Eternal Nature and Supreme Authority of God

The existence of God, His divine authority, and the origin of His name are profound questions that have captivated theologians, philosophers, and believers throughout history. These questions challenge us to contemplate the very essence of divinity and the nature of existence itself. How did God come into existence before He created the heavens and the earth? How did He give Himself the name "God"? Where did He get His authority?

These questions lead us to delve into the mysteries of God's omnipotence, sovereignty, and timelessness. They invite us to explore scriptural references, theological insights, and spiritual reflections to gain a comprehensive understanding of God's eternal existence and supreme authority. This chapter aims to set the stage for this exploration, providing a framework for understanding these profound concepts.

The Concept of God's Timeless Nature

One of the most challenging aspects of understanding God is His timeless nature. Unlike humans, who are bound by time and experience life in a linear progression, God exists outside of time. Psalm 90:2 declares, "Before the mountains were born or you brought forth the whole world, from everlasting to everlasting you are God." This verse emphasizes that God is eternal, having no beginning and no end. He exists from eternity past to eternity future, transcending the limitations of time.

The idea of God's timelessness is further supported by Revelation 1:8, where God is described as the Alpha and the Omega, the beginning and the end. This description highlights His eternal presence and His sovereign control over all of history. God's timeless nature means that He is always present, unchanging, and ever-reliable.

God's Self-Existence

Another key aspect of understanding God's nature is His self-existence or aseity. This concept means that God exists in and of Himself, independent of anything else. He is not created nor does He derive His existence from any other source. In Exodus 3:14, God reveals His name to Moses as "I AM WHO I AM." This name signifies God's self-existence and self-sufficiency. It declares that God is the ultimate being, whose existence is necessary and absolute.

God's self-existence is a foundational belief in Christian theology. It distinguishes Him from all created beings, who depend on God for their existence. God's aseity underscores His sovereignty and His ultimate authority over all creation. It means that He is the source of all life and being, and everything else exists by His will and power.

The Divine Authority of God

God's authority is intrinsic to His nature and is rooted in His role as the Creator of the universe. In the opening chapters of Genesis, we see God speaking the world into existence. His words carry creative power, bringing forth light, land, sea, and all living creatures. This act of creation demonstrates God's supreme authority over all things. He commands, and it comes to be.

God's authority is not just about power; it also involves His governance and moral order. Throughout the Bible, God establishes laws and principles that govern the behavior of His people. His commandments, given to Moses on Mount Sinai, provide a moral framework for human conduct. In the New Testament, Jesus' teachings further reveal the nature of God's authority, emphasizing love, justice, and mercy.

The authority of God is also evident in His ability to judge and to save. As the righteous judge, God holds the ultimate authority to determine the fate of His creation. His authority is just and righteous, rooted in His perfect nature. At the same time, God's authority is also seen in His redemptive work through Jesus Christ. Through Christ's sacrifice, God exercises His authority to offer salvation and eternal life to humanity.

The Mystery of God's Name

The name of God is more than just a label; it reveals His character and attributes. In the Bible, names carry significant meaning and often reflect the essence of a person. God's name, revealed as Yahweh or Jehovah in the Old Testament, signifies His eternal presence and His covenant relationship with His people. In Exodus 3:14-15, God tells Moses, "This is my name forever, the name you shall call me from generation to generation."

The name Yahweh, derived from the Hebrew verb "to be," encapsulates God's self-existence and eternal nature. It declares that He is the ever-present, unchanging God who remains faithful to His promises. Other names of God, such as El Shaddai (God Almighty) and Adonai (Lord), further reveal His power, sovereignty, and authority.

In the New Testament, the revelation of God's name continues with the coming of Jesus Christ. Jesus, whose name means "Yahweh saves," embodies the fullness of God's character and authority. Through His life, death, and resurrection, Jesus reveals the nature of God and His redemptive plan for humanity.

Understanding the Infinite

he human mind struggles to fully grasp the infinite nature of God. Our finite understanding is limited by our experiences and the constraints of time and space. However, faith calls us to trust in the truths revealed in scripture and to seek a deeper relationship with God. In Isaiah 55:8-9, God declares, "For my thoughts are not your thoughts, neither are your ways my ways. As the heavens are higher than the earth, so are my ways higher than your ways and my thoughts than your thoughts."

This passage reminds us that God's nature and ways are beyond our full comprehension. Yet, we are invited to trust in His wisdom, sovereignty, and love. Through faith, we can experience the transformative power of the everlasting God and gain a deeper understanding of His divine nature.

The questions of God's existence, His name, and His authority lead us to explore the profound mysteries of the divine. Through scriptural references, theological insights, and spiritual reflections, we can gain a deeper understanding of God's eternal existence, self-existence, and supreme authority. While these concepts may be challenging to fully grasp, they are central to our faith and our relationship with God.

As we embark on this journey of exploration, may we be inspired to trust in the everlasting God, whose power and presence can transform our lives and stories. Let us declare and decree that the power of the everlasting God will change our stories in Jesus' name. Amen.

DR. MAXWELL R. SHIMBA

CHAPTER 01

THE ETERNAL NATURE OF GOD

The eternal nature of God is a profound and foundational aspect of Christian theology. It is a concept that emphasizes God's existence outside the bounds of time and space, affirming that He is without beginning and without end. To fully appreciate this attribute, we must delve into the scriptures, analyze theological perspectives, and utilize tools such as exhaustive Strong's Concordance to understand the original meanings of key terms. This chapter will explore the eternal nature of God through an expository study, drawing upon biblical references and comprehensive commentary.

Scriptural Foundations of God's Eternal Nature

Psalm 90:2 provides a significant declaration of God's eternal nature: "Before the mountains were born or you brought forth the whole world, from everlasting to everlasting you are God." This verse presents the concept that God has existed eternally, from "everlasting to everlasting." The

Hebrew term used here, `olam (עוֹלָם), translated as "everlasting," denotes an infinite duration both backward and forward in time.

Another key verse is Isaiah 40:28, which states, "Do you not know? Have you not heard? The Lord is the everlasting God, the Creator of the ends of the earth. He will not grow tired or weary, and his understanding no one can fathom." The term used for "everlasting" here again emphasizes God's infinite existence and His unchanging nature.

Expository Study of Key Verses

Psalm 90:2

In Psalm 90:2, the phrase "from everlasting to everlasting" uses the Hebrew word `olam twice. According to Strong's Concordance (H5769), `olam means "long duration, antiquity, futurity, forever, ever, everlasting, evermore, perpetual, old, ancient, world." This repetition underscores the eternal aspect of God's existence, highlighting that He transcends all temporal bounds.

The commentary by Matthew Henry on this verse explains that God's existence before the formation of the earth and the universe signifies His supreme and eternal nature. He is the Creator who exists independently of His creation, affirming His self-sufficiency and sovereignty.

Isaiah 40:28

Isaiah 40:28 further elaborates on God's eternal nature and His inexhaustible power. The term "everlasting" (Hebrew `olam, H5769) here emphasizes God's eternal presence and His continuous activity in the world. The verse also points out that God's understanding is beyond human comprehension, indicating His infinite wisdom and knowledge.

John Gill's Exposition of the Entire Bible remarks that God's eternal nature is linked with His role as the Creator, emphasizing that His existence and authority extend beyond the confines of time and creation. God's eternal existence assures believers of His unchanging nature and His perpetual involvement in the world.

Theological Perspectives on God's Eternal Nature

The concept of God's eternal nature has been a central tenet in Christian theology. The Church Fathers, such as Augustine and Aquinas, emphasized God's timeless existence as an essential attribute of His divinity. Augustine, in his "Confessions," reflects on God's timeless nature, stating that God exists in an eternal present, where past, present, and future are all equally accessible to Him.

Thomas Aquinas, in his "Summa Theologica," argues that God's eternity is the fullness of existence, free from any temporal constraints. He explains that God's eternal nature means that He does not experience time as a succession of moments but exists in an unchanging, perpetual state.

The Eternal Nature of God in Systematic Theology

Systematic theology provides a structured approach to understanding God's eternal nature. The doctrine of divine eternity is closely related to God's immutability, meaning that God does not change over time. Malachi 3:6 declares, "I the Lord do not change. So you, the descendants of Jacob, are not destroyed." This immutability is a direct consequence of God's eternal nature; because God exists outside of time, He remains the same forever.

Furthermore, God's eternity is tied to His omnipresence and omniscience. Psalm 139:7-10 highlights God's omnipresence: "Where can I go from your Spirit? Where can I flee from your presence? If I go up to the heavens, you are there; if I make my bed in the depths, you are there. If I rise on the wings of the dawn, if I settle on the far side of the sea, even there your hand will guide me, your right hand will hold me fast." God's eternal nature means that He is present at all times and places, and His knowledge encompasses all events, past, present, and future.

Practical Implications of God's Eternal Nature

Understanding God's eternal nature has profound implications for believers. It provides assurance of God's unchanging character and His perpetual presence in our lives. In times of uncertainty and change, believers can find comfort in knowing that God remains constant. Hebrews 13:8 affirms this truth: "Jesus Christ is the same yesterday and today and forever."

God's eternal nature also assures us of His faithfulness. Lamentations 3:22-23 states, "Because of the Lord's great love we are not consumed, for his compassions never fail. They are new every morning; great is your faithfulness." This faithfulness is rooted in God's eternal nature; His promises are steadfast and reliable.

Moreover, God's eternal nature calls us to a life of eternal perspective. Colossians 3:2 encourages us to "Set your minds on things above, not on earthly things." Understanding that God is eternal and His kingdom is everlasting shifts our focus from temporary, worldly concerns to the eternal purposes and promises of God.

The eternal nature of God is a profound and essential aspect of His divine character. Through scriptural references, theological insights, and comprehensive commentary, we gain a deeper understanding of God's existence beyond the bounds of time. God's eternal nature assures us of His unchanging character, His perpetual presence, and His steadfast faithfulness. As we reflect on these truths, may we be inspired to live with an eternal perspective, trusting in the everlasting God who transcends time and remains sovereign over all creation.

In the words of Psalm 90:2, let us remember that "Before the mountains were born or you brought forth the whole world, from everlasting to everlasting you are God." This declaration of God's eternal nature invites us to trust in Him, to find comfort in His unchanging presence, and to live with the assurance that our God is eternal, sovereign, and ever-faithful.

Intrinsically, God's eternal nature is foundational to Christian theology and the understanding of the divine. As finite beings, our comprehension of eternity is limited by our experiences within time. Yet, the Bible reveals that God exists beyond these temporal constraints. He is described as the Alpha and the Omega, the First and the Last (Revelation 22:13), signifying His existence from eternity past to eternity future. This chapter explores the biblical basis, theological implications, and practical significance of God's eternal nature.

Understanding God's Eternal Nature

The Bible provides numerous references to God's eternal nature. One of the clearest statements is found in Psalm 90:2: "Before the mountains were born or you brought forth the whole world, from everlasting to everlasting you are God." This verse highlights God's existence before the creation of the world, emphasizing that He transcends the physical universe and its temporal limitations.

In the New Testament, Revelation 1:8 reiterates this truth: "'I am the Alpha and the Omega,' says the Lord God, 'who is, and who was, and who is to come, the Almighty.'" The terms Alpha and Omega, the first and last letters of the Greek alphabet, symbolize God's eternal presence and His sovereignty over all of history. This eternal existence is a unique attribute of God, distinguishing Him from all created beings and things.

Biblical Exegesis of Key Verses

Psalm 90:2

The phrase "from everlasting to everlasting" in Psalm 90:2 uses the Hebrew word `olam (עוֹלָם), which Strong's Concordance (H5769) defines as "long duration, antiquity, futurity, forever, ever, everlasting, perpetual, old, ancient." This repetition underscores the infinite nature of God's existence. The context of this psalm, attributed to Moses, reflects on the frailty of human life in contrast to God's eternal being. Moses acknowledges that God's existence precedes the formation of the earth, affirming His role as the eternal Creator.

Commentary from Matthew Henry emphasizes that God's eternal nature means He is unchanging and constant, providing a stable foundation for our faith. This understanding brings comfort and assurance, knowing that God's nature and promises remain steadfast throughout all generations.

Revelation 1:8

Revelation 1:8 offers a powerful declaration of God's eternal nature: "I am the Alpha and the Omega, says the Lord God, who is, and who was, and who is to come, the Almighty." The terms Alpha and Omega signify the completeness of God's existence, encompassing all of time and beyond. This verse not only affirms God's eternal nature but also His omnipotence, being described as "the Almighty."

John Gill's Exposition of the Entire Bible notes that this title signifies God's unchangeableness and eternal duration. It highlights that God is the beginning and the end of all things, underscoring His sovereignty and ultimate authority over creation.

Theological Implications of God's Eternal Nature

The doctrine of God's eternity is central to systematic theology and impacts our understanding of His other attributes. God's eternal nature is intrinsically linked to His immutability, the idea that God does not change. Malachi 3:6

states, "I the Lord do not change. So you, the descendants of Jacob, are not destroyed." This immutability provides believers with the assurance that God's character, promises, and purposes remain constant through all ages.

Additionally, God's eternal nature underscores His omnipresence and omniscience. Psalm 139:7-10 beautifully illustrates God's omnipresence: "Where can I go from your Spirit? Where can I flee from your presence? If I go up to the heavens, you are there; if I make my bed in the depths, you are there. If I rise on the wings of the dawn, if I settle on the far side of the sea, even there your hand will guide me, your right hand will hold me fast." God's presence and knowledge extend infinitely, unhindered by the passage of time or the boundaries of space.

Practical Significance of God's Eternal Nature

Understanding God's eternal nature has profound implications for our faith and daily lives. It provides a sense of stability and security, knowing that God is unchanging and ever-present. In times of uncertainty and change, we can trust in God's constancy. Hebrews 13:8 reassures us, "Jesus Christ is the same yesterday and today and forever."

God's eternal nature also calls us to live with an eternal perspective. Colossians 3:2 encourages believers to "Set your minds on things above, not on earthly things." Recognizing that our lives are part of a larger, eternal plan helps us prioritize spiritual growth and eternal values over temporary, worldly concerns.

Furthermore, the eternal nature of God invites us into a relationship with an everlasting, loving Creator. His eternal love and faithfulness are sources of immense comfort and hope. Lamentations 3:22-23 reminds us, "Because of the Lord's great love we are not consumed, for his compassions never fail. They are new every morning; great is your faithfulness."

The Mystery of God's Eternity

Despite our best efforts to understand God's eternal nature, it remains a profound mystery. Isaiah 55:8-9 captures this sentiment: "For my thoughts are not your thoughts, neither are your ways my ways, declares the Lord. As the heavens are higher than the earth, so are my ways higher than your ways and my thoughts than your thoughts." This passage reminds us that God's nature and ways are beyond our full comprehension, yet we are called to trust in His infinite wisdom and goodness.

Faith invites us to embrace the mystery of God's eternity, acknowledging our limited understanding while trusting in the revealed truths of scripture. Through faith, we can experience the transformative power of God's eternal nature, finding peace, purpose, and direction for our lives.

The eternal nature of God is a cornerstone of Christian belief, revealing His existence beyond the confines of time and space. Through biblical exegesis, theological reflection, and practical application, we gain a deeper appreciation of this divine attribute. God's eternal nature assures us of His unchanging character, His perpetual presence, and His steadfast faithfulness. As we contemplate these truths, may we be inspired to trust in the everlasting God and to live with an eternal perspective.

In the words of Revelation 1:8, let us remember that God is "the Alpha and the Omega, who is, and who was, and who is to come, the Almighty." This declaration invites us to anchor our faith in the eternal, sovereign, and ever-faithful God, whose love and presence transcend all time and creation.

The Eternal Nature and Name of God

The concept of God's eternal nature and the origin of His name are foundational to understanding His divine identity. The eternal nature of God signifies His existence beyond the constraints of time, affirming that He has no beginning and no end. Simultaneously, the name "God" and its significance offer profound insights into His character and essence. This chapter explores these themes, delving into biblical references, theological perspectives, and linguistic insights to provide a comprehensive understanding of God's eternal nature and the origin of His name.

The Eternal Nature of God

Understanding God's eternal nature is crucial for grasping His divinity. Psalm 90:2 states, "Before the mountains were born or you brought forth the whole world, from everlasting to everlasting you are God." This verse emphasizes that God exists outside of time, having no beginning or end. The Hebrew word used here, `olam (עוֹלָם), translates to "everlasting," indicating an infinite duration that stretches beyond human comprehension.

In Revelation 22:13, God declares, "I am the Alpha and the Omega, the First and the Last, the Beginning and the End." This statement underscores God's sovereignty over all time and creation. He is the origin and the culmination of everything, affirming His eternal presence and authority.

Biblical Exegesis of Key Verses

Psalm 90:2

Psalm 90:2 highlights God's existence before the creation of the physical universe: "Before the mountains were born or you brought forth the whole world, from everlasting to everlasting you are God." The repetition of `olam emphasizes God's eternal nature. This verse is part of a prayer attributed to Moses, reflecting on the transient nature of human life compared to God's eternal existence.

Matthew Henry's commentary on this verse emphasizes that God's eternity provides a stable foundation for our faith. Unlike humans, who experience life within the constraints of time, God exists in a perpetual, unchanging state.

Revelation 22:13

Revelation 22:13 presents a powerful declaration of God's eternal nature: "I am the Alpha and the Omega, the First and the Last, the Beginning and the End." The terms Alpha and Omega, the first and last letters of the Greek alphabet, symbolize God's eternal presence and His sovereignty over all history.

John Gill's Exposition of the Entire Bible explains that this title signifies God's unchangeableness and eternal duration. It underscores that God is the beginning and the end of all things, highlighting His ultimate authority and sovereignty over creation.

Theological Implications of God's Eternal Nature

The doctrine of God's eternity is central to systematic theology and impacts our understanding of His other attributes. God's eternal nature is intrinsically linked to His immutability, meaning that God does not change. Malachi 3:6 states, "I the Lord do not change. So you, the descendants of Jacob, are not destroyed." This immutability provides believers with the assurance that God's character, promises, and purposes remain constant through all ages.

Additionally, God's eternal nature underscores His omnipresence and omniscience. Psalm 139:7-10 beautifully illustrates God's omnipresence: "Where can I go from your Spirit? Where can I flee from your presence? If I go up to the heavens, you are there; if I make my bed in the depths, you are there. If I rise on the wings of the dawn, if I settle on the far side of the sea, even there your hand will guide me, your right hand will hold me fast." God's presence and knowledge extend infinitely, unhindered by the passage of time or the boundaries of space.

The Origin of the Name "God"

The name "God" carries deep significance and reflects the essence of the divine. The English word "God" originates from the Old English "god," which in turn derives from the Proto-Germanic guđán. This term is related to words in other Germanic languages, such as the Dutch "god" and the German "Gott." The etymology of "God" is linked to the Indo-European root ǵhu-tó-m, which means "that which is invoked" or "a being worthy of worship."

In the Hebrew Bible, the primary name for God is Elohim (אֱלֹהִים). Elohim is a plural noun used singularly when referring to the one true God, emphasizing His majesty and power. Another significant name is Yahweh (יהוה), revealed to Moses in Exodus 3:14-15: "God said to Moses, 'I AM WHO I AM. This is what you are to say to the Israelites: I AM has sent me to you.'" The name Yahweh, derived from the Hebrew verb "to be," signifies God's eternal, self-existent nature.

The name Yahweh is considered so sacred in Judaism that it is often replaced with Adonai (אֲדֹנָי), meaning "Lord," during readings of the Hebrew scriptures. This practice underscores the reverence and awe associated with the divine name.

Why "God" Means God

The term "God" encapsulates the attributes of divinity, authority, and worship. In theological discourse, "God" represents the supreme being who is all-powerful, all-knowing, and ever-present. The usage of "God" in different cultures and languages reflects the universal recognition of a higher power worthy of reverence and worship.

In Christian theology, God is understood as the Creator and Sustainer of the universe, the source of all life and existence. The name "God" signifies His ultimate authority and sovereign power. The Bible uses various names and titles to describe God, each revealing different aspects of His character and nature. For instance, El Shaddai (God Almighty) emphasizes His omnipotence, while Jehovah Jireh (The Lord Will Provide) highlights His provision and care for His people.

The use of the name "God" in prayers, hymns, and religious texts signifies a recognition of His divine nature and a call to worship and obedience. It reflects a relationship of reverence, trust, and dependence on the divine.

Practical Implications of God's Eternal Nature and Name

Understanding the eternal nature of God and the significance of His name has profound implications for our faith and daily lives. It provides a sense of stability and security, knowing that God is unchanging and ever-present. In times of uncertainty and change, we can trust in God's constancy. Hebrews 13:8 reassures us, "Jesus Christ is the same yesterday and today and forever."

God's eternal nature also calls us to live with an eternal perspective. Colossians 3:2 encourages believers to "Set your minds on things above, not on earthly things." Recognizing that our lives are part of a larger, eternal plan helps us prioritize spiritual growth and eternal values over temporary, worldly concerns.

Furthermore, the eternal nature of God invites us into a relationship with an everlasting, loving Creator. His eternal love and faithfulness are sources of immense comfort and hope. Lamentations 3:22-23 reminds us, "Because of the Lord's great love we are not consumed, for his compassions never fail. They are new every morning; great is your faithfulness."

The eternal nature of God and the origin of His name are profound aspects of His divine character. Through biblical exegesis, theological reflection, and linguistic insights, we gain a deeper understanding of God's existence beyond the bounds of time and the significance of His name. God's eternal nature assures us of His unchanging character, His perpetual presence, and His steadfast faithfulness. As we reflect on these truths, may we be inspired to trust in the everlasting God and to live with an eternal perspective.

In the words of Revelation 1:8, let us remember that God is "the Alpha and the Omega, who is, and who was, and who is to come, the Almighty." This declaration invites us to anchor our faith in the eternal, sovereign, and ever-faithful God, whose love and presence transcend all time and creation.

CHAPTER 02

GOD'S SELF-EXISTENCE

The self-existence of God, also known as His aseity, is a fundamental aspect of His divine nature. This concept refers to God's existence in and of Himself, independent of anything else. Unlike all created beings, who derive their existence from external sources, God is self-sufficient and self-sustaining. This chapter explores the biblical foundation, theological implications, and practical significance of God's self-existence, drawing on scriptural references and theological insights to provide a comprehensive understanding of this profound attribute.

Biblical Foundations of God's Self-Existence

The self-existence of God is clearly articulated in the Bible. One of the most significant passages is Exodus 3:14, where God reveals His name to Moses: "God said to Moses, 'I AM WHO I AM. This is what you are to say to the Israelites: I AM has sent me to you.'" The name "I AM" (Hebrew: אֶהְיֶה, Ehyeh) signifies God's self-existence and self-sufficiency. It indicates that God is the ground of His own being and does not depend on anything else for His existence.

Another key verse is John 5:26, where Jesus says, "For as the Father has life in himself, so he has granted the Son also to have life in himself." This verse emphasizes that God's life is inherent and not derived from any other source. The self-existence of God is also implied in Acts 17:24-25: "The God who made the world and everything in it is the Lord of heaven and earth and does not live in temples built by human hands. And he is not served by human hands, as if he needed anything. Rather, he himself gives everyone life and breath and everything else."

Expository Study of Key Verses

Exodus 3:14

In Exodus 3:14, God's declaration "I AM WHO I AM" reveals His self-existence. The Hebrew phrase אֶהְיֶה אֲשֶׁר אֶהְיֶה (Ehyeh Asher Ehyeh) can be translated as "I am who I am," "I will be what I will be," or "I am the One who is." This name indicates that God is the eternal, self-existing One who is the source of all being.

Strong's Concordance (H1961) defines אֶהְיֶה (Ehyeh) as "to be, to exist." This term underscores God's self-sustaining nature, affirming that He is not dependent on any external factors for His existence. The commentary by Matthew Henry explains that this name signifies God's immutability and faithfulness, as well as His self-existence. It assures us that God is the same throughout all ages and that His promises are reliable because they are rooted in His unchanging nature.

John 5:26

John 5:26 states, "For as the Father has life in himself, so he has granted the Son also to have life in himself." This verse highlights the inherent life within God. The Greek word for "life" (ζωή, zoe) in this context refers to the divine, uncreated life that God possesses. It is a life that is self-existent and not contingent upon anything else.

John Gill's Exposition of the Entire Bible notes that this verse affirms the deity of Christ, indicating that He shares the same self-existent life as the Father. It emphasizes the unity of the Father and the Son in possessing inherent, self-sustaining life, underscoring the divine nature of both.

Theological Implications of God's Self-Existence

The self-existence of God has significant theological implications. It affirms God's absolute independence and sovereignty. As the self-existent One, God is not subject to any external forces or influences. He is the ultimate source of all life and being, and everything else depends on Him for existence.

This attribute also underscores God's aseity, which means He is self-sufficient and self-contained. God's aseity implies that He is complete in Himself and lacks nothing. He does not need anything from His creation to fulfill or sustain Himself. This truth is reflected in Acts 17:24-25, where Paul explains that God is not served by human hands as if He needed anything. Instead, He is the giver of life and breath to all things.

God's self-existence also highlights His transcendence and immanence. As the self-existent Creator, God transcends His creation, existing independently of it. Yet, He is also immanent, actively sustaining and upholding all things. Colossians 1:17 states, "He is before all things, and in him all things hold together." This verse underscores that God's self-existent nature enables Him to sustain the universe and maintain its order.

Practical Significance of God's Self-Existence

Understanding God's self-existence has profound implications for our faith and daily lives. It provides a foundation for trusting in God's sovereignty and sufficiency. Since God is self-existent and independent, we can rely on Him completely, knowing that He is the ultimate source of life, provision, and strength.

God's self-existence also calls us to a posture of humility and dependence. Recognizing that we are contingent beings, reliant on God for our existence and sustenance, fosters a sense of humility and gratitude. It reminds us that our lives are not self-sustained but are upheld by the gracious and self-existent God.

Furthermore, God's self-existence assures us of His eternal and unchanging nature. Because God is self-existent, He remains constant and faithful throughout all ages. His promises are trustworthy, and His character is reliable. This assurance provides comfort and stability in an ever-changing world.

The Mystery of God's Self-Existence

Despite our efforts to understand God's self-existence, it remains a profound mystery. The finite human mind cannot fully grasp the concept of a being who exists independently and eternally. Isaiah 55:8-9 captures this reality: "For my thoughts are not your thoughts, neither are your ways my ways, declares the Lord. As the heavens are higher than the earth, so are my ways higher than your ways and my thoughts than your thoughts."

Faith invites us to embrace the mystery of God's self-existence, acknowledging our limited understanding while trusting in the revealed truths of scripture. Through faith, we can experience the transformative power of God's self-sufficient nature, finding peace, purpose, and direction for our lives.

The self-existence of God is a foundational aspect of His divine nature. Through biblical exegesis, theological reflection, and practical application, we gain a deeper understanding of God's aseity. God's self-existence affirms His independence, sovereignty, and sufficiency, providing a stable foundation for our faith. As we contemplate these truths, may we be inspired to trust in the self-existent God, to live with humility and dependence, and to find comfort in His unchanging and eternal nature.

In the words of Exodus 3:14, let us remember that God is "I AM WHO I AM." This declaration invites us to anchor our faith in the self-sufficient, sovereign, and ever-faithful God, who exists independently and sustains all creation.

Furthermore, God's self-existence, or aseity, is a reality that reveals the profound mystery and majesty of the divine. Unlike all created beings that depend on something else for their existence, God exists by His own power and will. This self-existence is foundational to understanding His divine nature and authority. It affirms that God is the ultimate source of all life and being, independent and self-sustaining. This chapter explores the biblical foundation, theological significance, and practical implications of God's self-existence.

Biblical Foundations of God's Self-Existence

The Bible clearly articulates the self-existence of God. One of the most pivotal passages is Exodus 3:14, where God reveals Himself to Moses: "God said to Moses, 'I AM WHO I AM. This is what you are to say to the Israelites: I AM has sent me to you.'" The name "I AM" (Hebrew: אֶהְיֶה, Ehyeh) signifies God's self-existence and self-sufficiency, indicating that He is the ground of His own being and does not depend on anything else.

Another significant verse is John 5:26, where Jesus says, "For as the Father has life in himself, so he has granted the Son also to have life in himself." This verse highlights the inherent life within God, emphasizing that His existence is not derived from any external source but is intrinsic to His nature.

Acts 17:24-25 further underscores God's independence: "The God who made the world and everything in it is the Lord of heaven and earth and does not live in temples built by human hands. And he is not served by human hands, as if he needed anything. Rather, he himself gives everyone life and breath and everything else." These verses emphasize that God is the giver of all life and is not dependent on His creation for anything.

Expository Study of Key Verses

Exodus 3:14

In Exodus 3:14, God's declaration "I AM WHO I AM" is profound. The Hebrew phrase אֶהְיֶה אֲשֶׁר אֶהְיֶה (Ehyeh Asher Ehyeh) can be translated as "I am who I am," "I will be what I will be," or "I am the One who is." This name reveals God's self-sustaining nature, affirming that He exists independently and eternally.

Strong's Concordance (H1961) defines אֶהְיֶה (Ehyeh) as "to be, to exist." This term underscores God's self-existence, highlighting that He is the ultimate source of His own being. Matthew Henry's commentary explains that this name signifies God's immutability and faithfulness, as well as His self-existence. It assures us that God is unchanging and reliable because His existence does not depend on anything outside of Himself.

John 5:26

John 5:26 states, "For as the Father has life in himself, so he has granted the Son also to have life in himself." This verse highlights the inherent life within God. The Greek word for "life" (ζωή, zoe) in this context refers to the divine, uncreated life that God possesses. It is a life that is self-existent and not contingent upon anything else.

John Gill's Exposition of the Entire Bible notes that this verse affirms the deity of Christ, indicating that He shares the same self-existent life as the Father. It emphasizes the unity of the Father and the Son in possessing inherent, self-sustaining life, underscoring the divine nature of both.

Acts 17:24-25

Acts 17:24-25 presents a clear declaration of God's self-sufficiency and independence: "The God who made the world and everything in it is the Lord of heaven and earth and does not live in temples built by human hands. And he is not served by human hands, as if he needed anything. Rather, he himself gives everyone life and breath and everything else." These verses emphasize that God is the creator and sustainer of all life, highlighting His self-sufficiency and independence from His creation.

The commentary by Albert Barnes on these verses explains that God's self-existence means He is not confined to human structures or dependent on human services. Instead, He is the provider of life and all its necessities, further affirming His sovereignty and self-sufficiency.

Theological Implications of God's Self-Existence

The self-existence of God has significant theological implications. It affirms God's absolute independence and sovereignty. As the self-existent One, God is not subject to any external forces or influences. He is the ultimate source of all life and being, and everything else depends on Him for existence.

This attribute also underscores God's aseity, meaning He is self-sufficient and self-contained. God's aseity implies that He is complete in Himself and lacks nothing. He does not need anything from His creation to fulfill or sustain Himself. This truth is reflected in Acts 17:24-25, where Paul explains that God is not served by human hands as if He needed anything. Instead, He is the giver of life and breath to all things.

God's self-existence also highlights His transcendence and immanence. As the self-existent Creator, God transcends His creation, existing independently of it. Yet, He is also immanent, actively sustaining and upholding all things.

Colossians 1:17 states, "He is before all things, and in him all things hold together." This verse underscores that God's self-existent nature enables Him to sustain the universe and maintain its order.

Practical Significance of God's Self-Existence

Understanding God's self-existence has profound implications for our faith and daily lives. It provides a foundation for trusting in God's sovereignty and sufficiency. Since God is self-existent and independent, we can rely on Him completely, knowing that He is the ultimate source of life, provision, and strength.

God's self-existence also calls us to a posture of humility and dependence. Recognizing that we are contingent beings, reliant on God for our existence and sustenance, fosters a sense of humility and gratitude. It reminds us that our lives are not self-sustained but are upheld by the gracious and self-existent God.

Furthermore, God's self-existence assures us of His eternal and unchanging nature. Because God is self-existent, He remains constant and faithful throughout all ages. His promises are trustworthy, and His character is reliable. This assurance provides comfort and stability in an ever-changing world.

The Mystery of God's Self-Existence

Despite our efforts to understand God's self-existence, it remains a profound mystery. The finite human mind cannot fully grasp the concept of a being who exists independently and eternally. Isaiah 55:8-9 captures this reality: "For my thoughts are not your thoughts, neither are your ways my ways, declares the Lord. As the heavens are higher than the earth, so are my ways higher than your ways and my thoughts than your thoughts."

Faith invites us to embrace the mystery of God's self-existence, acknowledging our limited understanding while trusting in the revealed truths of scripture. Through faith, we can experience the transformative power of God's self-sufficient nature, finding peace, purpose, and direction for our lives.

The self-existence of God is a foundational aspect of His divine nature. Through biblical exegesis, theological reflection, and practical application, we gain a deeper understanding of God's aseity. God's self-existence affirms His independence, sovereignty, and sufficiency, providing a stable foundation for our faith. As we contemplate these truths, may we be inspired to trust in the self-existent God, to live with humility and dependence, and to find comfort in His unchanging and eternal nature.

In the words of Exodus 3:14, let us remember that God is "I AM WHO I AM." This declaration invites us to anchor our faith in the self-sufficient, sovereign, and ever-faithful God, who exists independently and sustains all creation.

The Uncreated Creator

The concept of God as the Uncreated Creator is fundamental to understanding His divine nature and authority. Unlike all created beings, who derive their existence from something else, God exists by His own power and will. This self-existence and His role as the Creator of all things set Him apart as unique and supreme. This chapter explores what it means for God to be the Uncreated Creator, drawing from scriptural references, theological insights, and practical implications to offer a comprehensive understanding of this profound attribute.

The Meaning of the Uncreated Creator

To describe God as the Uncreated Creator is to affirm that He is the source of all existence while being Himself uncaused and independent. This concept underscores God's self-sufficiency and eternal nature. He is not a contingent being, meaning His existence does not depend on anything else. Instead, He is the necessary being who brought everything else into existence.

The term "Uncreated" signifies that God has no origin or beginning. Unlike everything in the universe, which came into being at some point, God always existed. The term "Creator" emphasizes His role in bringing the universe and all it contains into existence. Thus, the Uncreated Creator is a title that highlights both God's self-existence and His creative power.

Biblical Foundations of the Uncreated Creator

The Bible provides numerous references to God as the Uncreated Creator. One of the most explicit declarations is found in Genesis 1:1: "In the beginning, God created the heavens and the earth." This verse marks the commencement of time and space, initiated by God's creative act. It emphasizes that before anything else existed, God was already present.

John 1:1-3 further elaborates this concept: "In the beginning was the Word, and the Word was with God, and the Word was God. He was with God in the beginning. Through him all things were made; without him nothing was made that has been made." These verses affirm that all creation came into being through God, who Himself was not created.

Colossians 1:16-17 also underscores God's role as the Creator: "For in him all things were created: things in heaven and on earth, visible and invisible, whether thrones or powers or rulers or authorities; all things have been created through him and for him. He is before all things, and in him all things hold together." This passage highlights the preeminence of Christ in creation and His sustaining power over the universe.

Expository Study of Key Verses

Genesis 1:1

"In the beginning, God created the heavens and the earth." This foundational verse establishes God's role as the Creator of everything that exists. The Hebrew word for "created" (בָּרָא, bara) is used exclusively in the Bible to describe God's creative activity, indicating that creation is a divine act beyond human capability.

Strong's Concordance (H1254) defines בָּרָא (bara) as "to create, shape, form." This term underscores the power and sovereignty of God in bringing the universe into existence from nothing (ex nihilo). The commentary by Matthew Henry highlights that this creative act marks the beginning of time and space, initiated by God's will and power.

John 1:1-3

"In the beginning was the Word, and the Word was with God, and the Word was God. He was with God in the beginning. Through him all things were made; without him nothing was made that has been made." These verses identify

Jesus (the Word) as the agent of creation, affirming His divinity and preexistence.

The Greek word for "Word" (λόγος, logos) conveys the idea of divine reason and creative order. John Gill's Exposition of the Entire Bible explains that these verses emphasize the eternal existence of Christ and His integral role in creation. Christ is both uncreated and the creator of all things, reinforcing the concept of the Uncreated Creator.

Colossians 1:16-17

"For in him all things were created: things in heaven and on earth, visible and invisible, whether thrones or powers or rulers or authorities; all things have been created through him and for him. He is before all things, and in him all things hold together." This passage highlights Christ's supremacy over creation and His sustaining power.

The Greek word for "created" (κτίζω, ktizo) in this context signifies the formation and establishment of all things. The commentary by Albert Barnes notes that this verse underscores Christ's authority and preeminence in creation. It affirms that everything exists through Him and for His purposes, reflecting the divine order and intentionality behind creation.

Theological Implications of the Uncreated Creator

The concept of God as the Uncreated Creator has profound theological implications. It affirms God's absolute independence and sovereignty. As the Uncreated Creator, God is not subject to any external forces or influences. He is the ultimate source of all life and being, and everything else depends on Him for existence.

This attribute also underscores God's transcendence and immanence. As the Creator, God transcends His creation, existing independently of it. Yet, He is also immanent, actively sustaining and upholding all things. Acts 17:28 states, "For in him we live and move and have our being." This verse emphasizes our total dependence on God for existence and sustenance.

The self-existence and creative power of God also highlight His uniqueness and holiness. Isaiah 40:25-26 declares, "'To whom will you compare me? Or who is my equal?' says the Holy One. Lift up your eyes and look to the heavens: Who created all these? He who brings out the starry host one by one and calls forth each of them by name. Because of his great power and mighty strength, not one of them is missing." This passage underscores the incomparable nature of God as the Creator of the universe.

Practical Implications of God's Role as the Uncreated Creator

Understanding God as the Uncreated Creator has profound implications for our faith and daily lives. It provides a foundation for trusting in God's sovereignty and sufficiency. Since God is the ultimate source of all life and being, we can rely on Him completely, knowing that He holds all things in His hands.

This concept also calls us to worship and reverence. Recognizing that God is the Creator of everything inspires awe and devotion. Psalm 95:6 invites us, "Come, let us bow down in worship, let us kneel before the Lord our Maker." Worshiping God as the Uncreated Creator acknowledges His majesty and our dependence on Him.

Moreover, understanding God's role as the Uncreated Creator fosters a sense of purpose and meaning. If God intentionally created the universe and everything in it, our lives have inherent value and purpose. Ephesians 2:10 reminds us, "For we are God's handiwork, created in Christ Jesus to do good works, which God prepared in advance for us to do." This verse affirms that our existence is part of God's divine plan.

The Mystery of the Uncreated Creator

Despite our efforts to understand God as the Uncreated Creator, it remains a profound mystery. The finite human mind cannot fully grasp the concept of a being who exists independently and eternally while bringing everything else into existence. Isaiah 55:8-9 captures this reality: "For my thoughts are not your thoughts, neither are your ways my ways, declares the Lord. As the heavens are higher than the earth, so are my ways higher than your ways and my thoughts than your thoughts."

Faith invites us to embrace the mystery of God's self-existence and creative power, acknowledging our limited understanding while trusting in the revealed truths of scripture. Through faith, we can experience the transformative power of God's role as the Uncreated Creator, finding peace, purpose, and direction for our lives.

The concept of God as the Uncreated Creator is a foundational aspect of His divine nature. Through biblical exegesis, theological reflection, and practical application, we gain a deeper understanding of God's self-existence and creative power. God's role as the Uncreated Creator affirms His independence, sovereignty, and sufficiency, providing a stable foundation for our faith. As we contemplate these truths, may we be inspired to trust in the self-existent, sovereign, and ever-faithful God, who exists independently and sustains all creation.

In the words of Genesis 1:1, let us remember that "In the beginning, God created the heavens and the earth." This declaration invites us to anchor our faith in the Uncreated Creator, whose love and presence transcend all time and creation, and who alone is worthy of our worship and reverence.

The Word of God - Creator or Creation?

The nature of the Word of God is a profound theological concept that has significant implications for understanding the relationship between God and creation. Central to this discussion are two key questions: Is the Word of God a Creator or part of the creation? And is the Word of God eternal? This chapter aims to explore these questions through biblical exegesis, theological reflection, and practical application, providing a comprehensive understanding of the nature and role of the Word of God.

The Word of God as Creator

The Bible presents the Word of God not merely as a component of creation but as an active agent in creation. One of the most explicit affirmations of this is found in the prologue of the Gospel of John. John 1:1-3 states:

"In the beginning was the Word, and the Word was with God, and the Word was God. He was with God in the beginning. Through him all things were made; without him nothing was made that has been made."

These verses clearly indicate that the Word (Greek: λόγος, Logos) existed from the beginning, was with God, and was God. The Logos is directly involved in the act of creation, through whom all things were made. This positions the Word not as a part of creation, but as the Creator.

In Genesis 1, the act of creation is repeatedly described as God speaking things into existence: "And God said, 'Let there be light,' and there was light" (Genesis 1:3). The power of God's spoken Word is central to the creation narrative, emphasizing that creation comes into being through the divine Word.

Colossians 1:16-17 further supports this understanding:

"For in him all things were created: things in heaven and on earth, visible and invisible, whether thrones or powers or rulers or authorities; all things have been created through him and for him. He is before all things, and in him all things hold together."

This passage identifies Christ, the Word incarnate, as the agent of creation and the one who sustains all things. It reinforces the idea that the Word of God is fundamentally a Creator, not a part of creation.

The Word of God as Eternal

The question of whether the Word of God is eternal is intricately linked to the nature of God Himself. If the Word is truly God, then it must share in God's eternal nature. John 1:1 affirms this, stating that "In the beginning was the Word, and the Word was with God, and the Word was God." The use of "was" (ἦν, ēn) indicates continuous existence, implying that the Word has always been and always will be.

Further evidence of the eternality of the Word is found in Hebrews 1:2-3:

"But in these last days he has spoken to us by his Son, whom he appointed heir of all things, and through whom also he made the universe. The Son is the radiance of God's glory and the exact representation of his being, sustaining all things by his powerful word."

This passage identifies the Son, the incarnate Word, as the one through whom God made the universe and who sustains all things by His powerful word. The eternal nature of the Word is evident in His role as the sustainer of creation, an ongoing function that requires eternal existence.

Revelation 19:13 describes Christ as "The Word of God," reinforcing His eternal identity. The Word is not bound by time; instead, it transcends temporal limitations, being involved in both the creation and the ultimate consummation of all things.

Theological Implications of the Word as Creator and Eternal

Understanding the Word of God as both Creator and eternal has significant theological implications. It affirms the divinity of Christ, the Word incarnate, and His integral role in the divine plan of salvation. This recognition elevates the Word of God beyond mere spoken or written words to a divine person who embodies God's will and purpose.

This concept also underscores the unity and coherence of the Godhead. The Father, Son (the Word), and Holy Spirit are distinct persons yet fully one in essence and purpose. The Word's involvement in creation and its eternal nature highlight the interdependent work of the Trinity in the divine economy.

Furthermore, the eternal nature of the Word guarantees the reliability and permanence of God's promises. Isaiah 40:8 states, "The grass withers and the flowers fall, but the word of our God endures forever." The enduring nature of God's Word provides assurance to believers that God's promises are steadfast and unchanging.

Practical Implications for Believers

For believers, recognizing the Word of God as both Creator and eternal has profound practical implications. It calls for a deeper reverence and devotion to Christ, the living

Word. Understanding that Christ, the Word, is both the Creator and sustainer of life should inspire awe, worship, and a commitment to live according to His teachings.

This recognition also provides comfort and assurance. In a world of constant change and uncertainty, the eternal Word of God remains a firm foundation. Believers can trust in the constancy of God's Word, knowing that it is unchanging and eternally true. This trust extends to the written Scriptures, which bear witness to the living Word and convey His eternal truths.

Additionally, the eternal nature of the Word encourages believers to prioritize eternal values over temporal concerns. Colossians 3:2 exhorts, "Set your minds on things above, not on earthly things." By focusing on the eternal Word, believers can align their lives with God's eternal purposes, fostering spiritual growth and maturity.

The Mystery and Majesty of the Word

Despite our efforts to comprehend the full nature of the Word of God, it remains a profound mystery. The finite human mind cannot fully grasp the concept of an eternal, uncreated being who is both God and the agent of creation. Yet, this mystery invites us into a deeper relationship with God, where faith bridges the gap between understanding and belief.

Isaiah 55:8-9 captures the transcendence of God's ways: "For my thoughts are not your thoughts, neither are your ways my ways, declares the Lord. As the heavens are higher than the earth, so are my ways higher than your ways and my thoughts than your thoughts."

Faith invites us to embrace the mystery of the Word, acknowledging our limited understanding while trusting in the revealed truths of scripture. Through faith, we can experience the transformative power of the Word, finding peace, purpose, and direction for our lives.

The Word of God is both Creator and eternal. Through biblical exegesis, theological reflection, and practical application, we gain a deeper understanding of the Word's divine nature and role. As the Creator, the Word brings all things into existence and sustains them. As eternal, the Word transcends time and remains unchanging and true.

These truths invite us to trust in the living Word, Jesus Christ, and to live in alignment with His eternal purposes. In the words of John 1:1-3, let us remember that "In the beginning was the Word, and the Word was with God, and the Word was God. Through him all things were made; without him nothing was made that has been made."

This declaration invites us to anchor our faith in the eternal, sovereign, and ever-faithful Word of God, who alone is worthy of our worship and reverence. As we reflect on these truths, may we be inspired to trust in the Word, to live with an eternal perspective, and to find comfort in the unchanging promises of God.

CHAPTER 03

THE NAME OF GOD

The name of God holds profound significance and power within biblical theology. Names in the Bible are often more than mere identifiers; they convey the nature, character, and essence of the individuals they describe. The name of God, as revealed to Moses in Exodus 3:14, is no exception. When God introduces Himself as "I AM WHO I AM," He reveals His eternal, self-existent, and sovereign nature. This chapter explores the depth and implications of God's name, drawing on scriptural references, theological insights, and practical applications to provide a comprehensive understanding of this pivotal revelation.

The Revelation of God's Name

In Exodus 3:14, during the encounter at the burning bush, God reveals His name to Moses: "God said to Moses, 'I AM WHO I AM. This is what you are to say to the Israelites: I AM has sent me to you.'" The Hebrew phrase used here is אֶהְיֶה אֲשֶׁר אֶהְיֶה (Ehyeh Asher Ehyeh), which can be translated as "I am who I am," "I will be what I will be," or "I am the One who is."

This name, often rendered as Yahweh (יהוה) or Jehovah in English translations, encapsulates the essence of God's eternal and self-existent nature. It signifies that God is unchanging, ever-present, and sovereign over all creation. The name Yahweh is derived from the Hebrew verb "to be" (הָיָה, hayah), emphasizing God's existence and presence.

The Significance of Yahweh

The name Yahweh is used extensively throughout the Old Testament, appearing over 6,800 times. It is often translated as "LORD" (in all capital letters) in English Bibles to distinguish it from the title "Lord" (Adonai). Yahweh is God's personal name, signifying His unique identity and relationship with His people.

Yahweh is first introduced in Genesis 2:4, where the creation account refers to "the LORD God" (Yahweh Elohim). This combination of Yahweh with Elohim (a more general term for God) emphasizes both God's personal nature and His role as the Creator. The use of Yahweh in the context of God's covenant with Israel further highlights His faithfulness and relational commitment to His people.

Biblical Exegesis of Key Verses

Exodus 3:14-15

"God said to Moses, 'I AM WHO I AM. This is what you are to say to the Israelites: I AM has sent me to you.' God also said to Moses, 'Say to the Israelites, "The LORD, the God of your fathers—the God of Abraham, the God of Isaac and the God of Jacob—has sent me to you." This is my name forever, the name you shall call me from generation to generation.'"

In this passage, God's self-revelation as "I AM WHO I AM" establishes His eternal and unchanging nature. The phrase אֶהְיֶה אֲשֶׁר אֶהְיֶה (Ehyeh Asher Ehyeh) underscores God's independence and self-sufficiency. He is not defined or limited by anything outside Himself.

Matthew Henry's commentary on this passage notes that God's name reveals His immutability and faithfulness. God's promise to be with His people is grounded in His eternal, unchanging nature, providing assurance and stability.

Exodus 6:2-3

"God also said to Moses, 'I am the LORD. I appeared to Abraham, to Isaac and to Jacob as God Almighty, but by my name the LORD I did not make myself fully known to them.'"

In this passage, God distinguishes between His revelation as "God Almighty" (El Shaddai) to the patriarchs and His revelation as "the LORD" (Yahweh) to Moses and the Israelites. This distinction highlights the progressive nature of God's self-revelation and His deepening relationship with His people.

John Gill's Exposition of the Bible explains that while the patriarchs were aware of the name Yahweh, the full significance and implications of this name were not fully revealed to them. God's revelation of His name to Moses signifies a deeper understanding of His nature and His covenant relationship with Israel.

Theological Implications of God's Name

The revelation of God's name Yahweh has profound theological implications. It affirms God's self-existence, sovereignty, and relational nature. These attributes are foundational to understanding God's character and His interactions with humanity.

Self-Existence and Immutability

God's self-existence (aseity) is encapsulated in the name Yahweh. As "I AM WHO I AM," God is the source of His own being, independent and uncaused. This self-existence underscores His immutability, meaning He does not change over time. Malachi 3:6 states, "I the LORD do not change. So you, the descendants of Jacob, are not destroyed." God's unchanging nature provides stability and reliability for His people.

Sovereignty and Authority

The name Yahweh also affirms God's sovereignty and ultimate authority. As the self-existent Creator, God holds supreme power over all creation. Isaiah 45:5-7 declares, "I am the LORD, and there is no other; apart from me there is no God. I will strengthen you, though you have not acknowledged me, so that from the rising of the sun to the place of its setting people may know there is none besides me. I am the LORD, and there is no other. I form the light and create darkness, I bring prosperity and create disaster; I, the LORD, do all these things."

Relational Nature

God's use of the name Yahweh in His covenant with Israel highlights His relational nature. He is not a distant, impersonal deity but a God who desires a personal relationship with His people. Exodus 34:6-7 reveals God's character in this relational context: "And he passed in front of Moses, proclaiming, 'The LORD, the LORD, the compassionate and gracious God, slow to anger, abounding in love and faithfulness, maintaining love to thousands, and forgiving wickedness, rebellion and sin. Yet he does not leave the guilty unpunished; he punishes the children and their children for the sin of the parents to the third and fourth generation.'"

Practical Implications for Believers

Understanding the significance of God's name has profound practical implications for believers. It deepens our reverence and worship, strengthens our faith, and informs our relationship with God.

Worship and Reverence

Recognizing the holiness and significance of God's name Yahweh inspires awe and worship. Psalm 8:1 proclaims, "LORD, our Lord, how majestic is your name in all the earth!" Worshiping God by His revealed name acknowledges His majesty and honors His character.

Trust and Dependence

The revelation of God's unchanging and sovereign nature through His name provides a solid foundation for trust. Believers can depend on God's faithfulness, knowing that He is the same yesterday, today, and forever (Hebrews

13:8). This assurance fosters a deeper reliance on God in all circumstances.

Relational Intimacy

Understanding God's desire for a personal relationship, as conveyed through His name Yahweh, encourages believers to seek a closer walk with Him. James 4:8 invites us, "Come near to God and he will come near to you." Knowing that God is compassionate, gracious, and abounding in love strengthens our commitment to pursuing intimacy with Him.

The Mystery and Majesty of God's Name

Despite our efforts to comprehend the full significance of God's name, it remains a profound mystery. The finite human mind cannot fully grasp the depth and majesty of the divine name Yahweh. Yet, this mystery invites us into a deeper relationship with God, where faith bridges the gap between understanding and belief.

Isaiah 55:8-9 captures the transcendence of God's ways: "For my thoughts are not your thoughts, neither are your ways my ways, declares the LORD. As the heavens are higher than the earth, so are my ways higher than your ways and my thoughts than your thoughts."

Faith invites us to embrace the mystery of God's name, acknowledging our limited understanding while trusting in the revealed truths of scripture. Through faith, we can experience the transformative power of God's name, finding peace, purpose, and direction for our lives.

The name of God, Yahweh, holds significant meaning and power, revealing His eternal, self-existent, and sovereign nature. Through biblical exegesis, theological reflection, and practical application, we gain a deeper understanding of the profound implications of God's name. As we contemplate these truths, may we be inspired to trust in the unchanging, sovereign, and ever-faithful God, whose name is above all names.

In the words of Exodus 3:15, let us remember that "The LORD, the God of your fathers—the God of Abraham, the God of Isaac and the God of Jacob—has sent me to you. This is my name forever, the name you shall call me from generation to generation." This declaration invites us to anchor our faith in Yahweh, the eternal and relational God, who alone is worthy of our worship and reverence.

The Names of God

Throughout the Bible, various names and titles are used to describe God, each revealing different aspects of His character and attributes. These names are not mere labels but profound revelations of His divine nature and His interaction with humanity. Understanding these names helps us to know

God more intimately and appreciate the depth of His relationship with His creation. This chapter explores some of the most significant names of God, such as El Shaddai, Adonai, and Elohim, and their theological and practical implications.

The Significance of God's Names

The names of God in the Bible serve as a window into His nature and character. They reveal His attributes, such as power, authority, and relational qualities. Each name highlights a different aspect of who God is and how He relates to His people. The importance of these names is underscored by their frequent use in prayer, worship, and scripture.

In the ancient Near East, names held great significance and were believed to convey the essence of a person's identity. This cultural context helps us understand why God's names are so important in the Bible. They are not arbitrary; each name carries deep meaning and reflects God's multifaceted nature.

El Shaddai (God Almighty)

The name El Shaddai (שַׁדַּי אֵל) is often translated as "God Almighty." It emphasizes God's ultimate power and authority over all creation. The name El Shaddai first appears in Genesis 17:1, where God says to Abram, "I am God Almighty; walk before me and be blameless."

The Hebrew word "El" means "God" and is used to denote deity. "Shaddai" is often understood to mean "Almighty" or "All-Sufficient." Together, El Shaddai conveys the idea of God being the supreme, powerful deity who is more than sufficient to meet all needs and fulfill all promises.

El Shaddai is used in contexts that emphasize God's power and ability to accomplish His purposes. For instance, in Genesis 28:3, Isaac blesses Jacob, saying, "May God Almighty bless you and make you fruitful and increase your numbers until you become a community of peoples." This blessing highlights God's power to bring about His promises of prosperity and growth.

Adonai (Lord)

The name Adonai (אֲדֹנָי) is translated as "Lord" and is used to express God's lordship and authority. It is a plural form of the Hebrew word "adon" (lord or master), which emphasizes God's supreme authority and governance. Adonai is often used in prayers and scriptures to denote reverence and submission to God's will.

One of the most notable uses of Adonai is found in Isaiah 6:1, where Isaiah has a vision of the Lord: "In the year that King Uzziah died, I saw the Lord, high and exalted, seated on a throne; and the train of his robe filled the temple." Here, Adonai is depicted as the sovereign ruler, exalted above all earthly authorities.

The name Adonai conveys the relationship between God and His people as one of master and servant. It calls believers to recognize God's authority in their lives and to submit to His guidance and commandments. This submission is not out of fear, but out of trust in God's wisdom and love.

Elohim (God)

Elohim (אֱלֹהִים) is a plural form of the Hebrew word "Eloah" (God) and is one of the most common names for God in the Old Testament. It appears in the very first verse of the Bible: "In the beginning, God (Elohim) created the heavens and the earth" (Genesis 1:1). The use of the plural form "Elohim" has been interpreted in various ways, including as a majestic plural or as an indication of the plurality within the Godhead, which aligns with the Christian doctrine of the Trinity.

Elohim emphasizes God's power as the Creator and His sovereignty over the universe. The name is used in contexts that highlight God's creative and sustaining power. For instance, in Psalm 19:1, it is written, "The heavens declare the glory of God; the skies proclaim the work of his hands." This verse underscores God's majesty and creative authority.

Elohim also signifies God's role as the judge and ruler of the world. In Deuteronomy 10:17, Moses declares, "For the LORD your God is God of gods and Lord of lords, the great God, mighty and awesome, who shows no partiality and accepts no bribes." This usage highlights God's supreme authority and impartial justice.

Other Significant Names of God

Yahweh (Jehovah)

The name Yahweh (יהוה) is often rendered as Jehovah in English translations. It is derived from the Hebrew verb "to be" (הָיָה, hayah) and is closely linked to the name revealed to Moses in Exodus 3:14, "I AM WHO I AM." Yahweh is considered the most sacred and personal name of God, emphasizing His eternal existence and faithfulness.

Yahweh is used extensively throughout the Old Testament to signify God's covenant relationship with His people. For instance, in Exodus 6:6-7, God promises, "I am the LORD, and I will bring you out from under the yoke of the Egyptians... I will take you as my own people, and I will be your God." This name highlights God's commitment to His people and His active involvement in their deliverance and sanctification.

Jehovah-Jireh (The Lord Will Provide)

Jehovah-Jireh (יְרָאֶה יהוה) means "The Lord Will Provide" and is first used in Genesis 22:14, where Abraham names the place where God provided a ram for the sacrifice in place of his son Isaac. "So Abraham called that place The LORD Will Provide. And to this day it is said, 'On the mountain of the LORD it will be provided.'"

This name underscores God's provision and care for His people. It reassures believers that God sees their needs and provides for them according to His riches and glory. This aspect of God's character encourages trust and reliance on Him in times of need.

El Elyon (God Most High)

El Elyon (אֵל עֶלְיוֹן) means "God Most High" and emphasizes God's supreme sovereignty and majesty. It is used in contexts that highlight God's exalted position above all other powers and authorities. For example, in Genesis 14:18-20, Melchizedek, the king of Salem, is described as "priest of God Most High," and he blesses Abram, saying, "Blessed be Abram by God Most High, Creator of heaven and earth. And praise be to God Most High, who delivered your enemies into your hand."

El Elyon signifies God's ultimate authority and His supremacy over all other gods and kings. It calls believers to recognize and worship God as the highest and most powerful being in the universe.

Jehovah-Rapha (The Lord Who Heals)

Jehovah-Rapha (רפא יהוה) means "The Lord Who Heals" and is found in Exodus 15:26, where God declares, "If you listen carefully to the LORD your God and do what is right in his eyes, if you pay attention to his commands and keep all his decrees, I will not bring on you any of the diseases I brought on the Egyptians, for I am the LORD, who heals you."

This name reveals God's power to heal and restore. It underscores His compassion and desire to bring wholeness to His people, both physically and spiritually. Believers can find comfort and hope in Jehovah-Rapha, trusting in His ability to heal and renew.

Theological Implications of God's Names

The various names of God reveal different aspects of His character and how He relates to His creation. Understanding these names enhances our theological knowledge and deepens our relationship with God.

God's Power and Authority

Names like El Shaddai and El Elyon emphasize God's supreme power and authority. They remind us that God is all-powerful and sovereign over all creation. This knowledge provides assurance and confidence, knowing that nothing is beyond God's control.

God's Relational Nature

Names like Yahweh and Adonai highlight God's desire for a personal relationship with His people. They reveal His faithfulness, compassion, and commitment to His covenant. Understanding these names helps us appreciate God's intimate involvement in our lives and His loving care for us.

God's Provision and Healing

Names like Jehovah-Jireh and Jehovah-Rapha reveal God's provision and healing power. They encourage us to trust in God's ability to meet our needs and to heal our brokenness. These names remind us of God's active presence in our lives and His ongoing work of restoration and renewal.

Practical Implications for Believers

Understanding the names of God has profound practical implications for believers. It deepens our worship, strengthens our faith, and informs our daily walk with God.

Deepening Worship

Recognizing the significance of God's names enhances our worship. Each name reveals a different aspect of God's character, inviting us to worship Him more fully. For example, acknowledging God as El Shaddai leads us to praise

Him for His power and might, while recognizing Him as Jehovah-Jireh inspires gratitude for His provision.

Strengthening Faith

The names of God provide a foundation for trust and faith. Understanding that God is El Elyon, the Most High, reassures us that He is in control of all circumstances. Knowing Him as Jehovah-Rapha encourages us to trust in His healing power. Each name strengthens our faith by revealing more of who God is and what He can do.

Informing Daily Walk

The names of God guide our daily walk with Him. They remind us of His presence, provision, and guidance. Recognizing God as Adonai calls us to submit to His lordship and follow His commands. Understanding Him as Yahweh, the covenant-keeping God, reassures us of His faithfulness in our daily lives.

The Mystery and Majesty of God's Names

Despite our efforts to understand the full significance of God's names, they remain a profound mystery. The finite human mind cannot fully grasp the depth and majesty of the divine. Yet, this mystery invites us into a deeper relationship with God, where faith bridges the gap between understanding and belief.

Isaiah 55:8-9 captures the transcendence of God's ways: "For my thoughts are not your thoughts, neither are your ways my ways, declares the LORD. As the heavens are higher than the earth, so are my ways higher than your ways and my thoughts than your thoughts."

Faith invites us to embrace the mystery of God's names, acknowledging our limited understanding while trusting in the revealed truths of scripture. Through faith, we can experience the transformative power of God's character, finding peace, purpose, and direction for our lives.

The names of God hold significant meaning and power, revealing different aspects of His character and attributes. Through biblical exegesis, theological reflection, and practical application, we gain a deeper understanding of the profound implications of God's names. As we contemplate these truths, may we be inspired to trust in the unchanging, sovereign, and ever-faithful God, whose names are above all names.

In the words of Psalm 9:10, let us remember that "Those who know your name trust in you, for you, LORD, have never forsaken those who seek you." This declaration invites us to anchor our faith in the God who reveals Himself through His many names, each reflecting His power, authority, and relational nature.

Are the Names of God God?

The names of God in the Bible hold profound significance and power, each revealing different aspects of His character and attributes. But a deeper question arises: are the names of God, God Himself? This chapter explores the nature and implications of God's names, examining whether these names are merely descriptors or if they encapsulate the very essence of God. Through biblical exegesis, theological reflection, and practical application, we aim to understand the relationship between God's names and His divine nature.

The Significance of God's Names

In biblical theology, names are not merely labels but convey the essence of a person's identity. This cultural understanding is particularly significant when it comes to the names of God. Each name of God in the Bible reveals specific aspects of His character, His actions, and His relationship with His creation.

The Hebrew tradition of naming reflects a deeper meaning and connection between the name and the nature of the person or entity. In the case of God, His names are a revelation of His divine attributes and His relationship with humanity. Names like El Shaddai (God Almighty), Adonai (Lord), and Yahweh (I AM) are not just titles; they are profound revelations of who God is.

Biblical Exegesis of Key Names

Yahweh (יהוה)

Yahweh, often rendered as Jehovah in English, is one of the most sacred names of God. It is first revealed in Exodus 3:14-15 when God speaks to Moses from the burning bush:

"God said to Moses, 'I AM WHO I AM. This is what you are to say to the Israelites: I AM has sent me to you.' God also said to Moses, 'Say to the Israelites, "The LORD, the God of your fathers—the God of Abraham, the God of Isaac and the God of Jacob—has sent me to you." This is my name forever, the name you shall call me from generation to generation.'"

The name Yahweh, derived from the Hebrew verb "to be," signifies God's eternal existence, self-sufficiency, and unchanging nature. It encapsulates the essence of God's being and His covenant relationship with His people. The name itself is considered so sacred that traditional Jewish practice avoids vocalizing it, using "Adonai" (Lord) instead.

Elohim (אֱלֹהִים)

Elohim is another significant name used for God, appearing over 2,500 times in the Old Testament. It is a plural noun used singularly to denote the one true God, emphasizing

His majesty and power. Genesis 1:1 introduces God as Elohim:

"In the beginning, God created the heavens and the earth."

The plural form of Elohim hints at the complexity and fullness of God's nature, aligning with the Christian understanding of the Trinity. Elohim as Creator highlights His sovereign power and authority over all creation. The use of Elohim signifies not just a title but an aspect of God's divine essence.

El Shaddai (שַׁדַּי אֵל)

El Shaddai, translated as "God Almighty," emphasizes God's ultimate power and sufficiency. It appears in Genesis 17:1:

"When Abram was ninety-nine years old, the LORD appeared to him and said, 'I am God Almighty; walk before me faithfully and be blameless.'"

El Shaddai conveys God's ability to fulfill His promises and His might in overcoming any obstacle. This name reflects an attribute of God's power and care, integral to understanding His character.

Adonai (אֲדֹנָי)

Adonai, meaning "Lord" or "Master," denotes God's authority and lordship. It expresses the relationship between

God and His people as one of a master to servants. Isaiah 6:1 depicts a vision of God as Adonai:

"In the year that King Uzziah died, I saw the Lord, high and exalted, seated on a throne; and the train of his robe filled the temple."

Adonai emphasizes God's sovereignty and His rightful authority over all creation. It is a name that calls for reverence and submission.

Are the Names of God God?

To address whether the names of God are God Himself, we must consider the nature of divine revelation. In revealing His names, God is not merely providing titles but is disclosing aspects of His very being. Each name of God reveals His essence, attributes, and relational dynamics with humanity. However, it is essential to understand that the names themselves are not separate entities but are integral to who God is.

The Revelation of God's Essence

When God reveals His name as Yahweh, He is not only providing a name but revealing His eternal and self-existent nature. The name Yahweh is synonymous with God's very being. Similarly, Elohim, El Shaddai, and Adonai are revelations of God's attributes and nature. They are not just descriptors but encapsulate aspects of God's essence.

Theological Reflections

Theologically, the names of God are seen as part of His self-revelation to humanity. They are means by which finite humans can begin to understand the infinite and transcendent nature of God. The names of God are windows into His character and being. They are not independent of God but are deeply connected to who He is.

John 1:1-2 provides an essential insight into this concept: "In the beginning was the Word, and the Word was with God, and the Word was God. He was with God in the beginning." Here, the Word (Logos) is identified as both with God and as God, emphasizing that divine revelation is not separate from God but is a part of His very essence.

Practical Implications for Believers

Understanding that the names of God are integral to His essence has profound implications for believers. It shapes our worship, strengthens our faith, and informs our relationship with God.

Worship and Reverence

Recognizing that the names of God reveal His very nature deepens our worship. Each name invites us to contemplate different aspects of God's character, leading to a more profound reverence and awe. Worshiping God by His names acknowledges His multifaceted nature and honors His divine attributes.

Strengthening Faith

The names of God provide a foundation for trust and confidence in Him. Knowing God as El Shaddai (God Almighty) reassures us of His power to act in our lives. Understanding Him as Yahweh (I AM) comforts us with His eternal presence and faithfulness. Each name strengthens our faith by revealing more of who God is.

Relational Intimacy

God's names reveal His desire for a relationship with His people. Names like Adonai (Lord) and Yahweh (I AM) emphasize His covenantal relationship and His commitment to His people. Understanding these names encourages believers to seek a closer walk with God, knowing He is both sovereign and intimately involved in their lives.

The names of God in the Bible are not just labels but profound revelations of His divine nature and attributes. They encapsulate the essence of who God is and how He relates to His creation. Each name, whether Yahweh, Elohim, El Shaddai, or Adonai, reveals a different facet of God's character and being.

Understanding that the names of God are integral to His essence deepens our worship, strengthens our faith, and informs our relationship with Him. These names are not separate entities but are deeply connected to the very nature of God. They are windows into His character, inviting us to know Him more intimately and worship Him more profoundly.

As we reflect on the names of God, let us be inspired to trust in the unchanging, sovereign, and ever-faithful God, whose names are a testament to His divine nature and His relational commitment to His people. In the words of Psalm 9:10, "Those who know your name trust in you, for you, LORD, have never forsaken those who seek you." This declaration invites us to anchor our faith in the God who reveals Himself through His many names, each reflecting His power, authority, and relational nature.

Are the Attributes of God, God?

The attributes of God, such as His omnipotence, omniscience, omnipresence, and immutability, are fundamental aspects of His nature. These attributes are often discussed in theological studies to understand better who God is and how He interacts with the world. But a deeper question arises: Are the attributes of God, God Himself? This chapter explores whether God's attributes are merely descriptions of His character or if they are integral to His very being, examining their biblical foundations, theological significance, and practical implications.

The Nature of God's Attributes

The attributes of God are essential qualities that define His nature and character. They are often categorized into communicable and incommunicable attributes. Communicable attributes are those that humans can reflect to some extent, such as love, mercy, and justice. Incommunicable attributes are unique to God, such as omnipotence, omniscience, and immutability.

Understanding these attributes helps us to grasp the fullness of God's nature. However, the question remains whether these attributes are simply aspects of God or if they embody God Himself.

Biblical Foundations of God's Attributes

The Bible provides numerous references to the attributes of God, revealing His nature and character through His actions and declarations.

Omnipotence

God's omnipotence, or all-powerfulness, is a key attribute that underscores His ability to do anything consistent with His nature. Genesis 18:14 states, "Is anything too hard for the LORD? I will return to you at the appointed time next year, and Sarah will have a son." This rhetorical question highlights God's unlimited power.

Revelation 19:6 also proclaims, "For our Lord God Almighty reigns." The term "Almighty" (Greek: παντοκράτωρ, pantokratōr) emphasizes God's supreme power over all things.

Omniscience

God's omniscience refers to His all-knowing nature. Psalm 147:5 declares, "Great is our Lord and mighty in power; his understanding has no limit." This verse highlights the infinite scope of God's knowledge.

1 John 3:20 also affirms, "If our hearts condemn us, we know that God is greater than our hearts, and he knows everything." God's omniscience encompasses all things, past, present, and future.

Omnipresence

God's omnipresence means that He is present everywhere at all times. Psalm 139:7-10 beautifully captures this attribute:

"Where can I go from your Spirit? Where can I flee from your presence? If I go up to the heavens, you are there; if I make my bed in the depths, you are there. If I rise on the wings of the dawn, if I settle on the far side of the sea, even there your hand will guide me, your right hand will hold me fast."

Jeremiah 23:24 also states, "Can anyone hide in secret places so that I cannot see him?" declares the LORD. "Do not I fill heaven and earth?" declares the LORD."

Immutability

God's immutability means that He does not change. Malachi 3:6 declares, "I the LORD do not change. So you, the descendants of Jacob, are not destroyed." This attribute assures us that God's nature and promises remain constant.

James 1:17 further emphasizes this, stating, "Every good and perfect gift is from above, coming down from the Father of the heavenly lights, who does not change like shifting shadows."

Are the Attributes of God God?

To address whether the attributes of God are God Himself, we must consider the nature of divine simplicity. The doctrine of divine simplicity asserts that God is not composed of parts but is entirely unified in His being. This means that God's attributes are not separate components but are fully integrated into His essence.

The Doctrine of Divine Simplicity

Divine simplicity means that God is not a composite being made up of different parts. Instead, He is entirely unified and indivisible. This doctrine asserts that God's attributes are identical to His essence. For instance, God does not possess love as a quality separate from His being; rather, God is love (1 John 4:8). Similarly, God does not possess power; He is power.

Thomas Aquinas, a prominent theologian, articulated this doctrine by stating that in God, "existence and essence are one and the same." This means that God's attributes are not additional qualities but are identical with His essence. Thus, God's omnipotence, omniscience, omnipresence, and immutability are not attributes He possesses but are who He is.

Biblical Support for Divine Simplicity

The Bible supports the idea that God's attributes are integral to His essence. For example, 1 John 4:8 states, "Whoever does not love does not know God, because God is love." This verse does not merely say that God is loving but that He is love itself, indicating that love is an essential part of God's nature.

Similarly, John 14:6 records Jesus saying, "I am the way and the truth and the life. No one comes to the Father except through me." Here, Jesus identifies Himself as the embodiment of truth and life, suggesting that these attributes are not external to God but are His very nature.

Theological Implications of Divine Simplicity

Understanding that God's attributes are God Himself has profound theological implications. It reinforces the unity and indivisibility of God's nature, ensuring that His attributes are not compartmentalized but are fully integrated into His being.

Unity of God's Nature

The doctrine of divine simplicity ensures that God's nature is perfectly unified. His love, justice, mercy, and power are not separate aspects but are harmoniously integrated into His essence. This unity means that all of God's actions are consistent with His nature. When God exercises justice, it is a loving justice. When He shows mercy, it is a powerful mercy. There is no conflict or division within God's nature.

Assurance of God's Promises

Understanding that God's attributes are integral to His essence provides assurance of His promises. Since God is unchanging (immutable), His promises remain steadfast. Because He is all-knowing (omniscient), He is fully aware of our needs and circumstances. His omnipotence ensures that He has the power to fulfill His promises, and His omnipresence means He is always with us.

Deepened Worship

Recognizing that God's attributes are God Himself deepens our worship. It leads us to worship God not just for what He does but for who He is. We can worship God for His love, knowing that He is love itself. We can praise Him for His power, understanding that He is the source of all power. This holistic understanding of God's nature enriches our worship and devotion.

Practical Implications for Believers

Understanding that the attributes of God are God Himself has practical implications for believers. It shapes our faith, informs our prayers, and guides our daily walk with God.

Strengthened Faith

Knowing that God's attributes are integral to His essence strengthens our faith. We can trust in God's unchanging nature, confident that His promises are reliable. We can rely on His omnipotence, knowing that He has the power to accomplish His will. This understanding fosters a deeper trust and confidence in God's character.

Informed Prayer

Understanding God's attributes informs our prayers. When we pray, we can appeal to God's omniscience, trusting that He knows our needs even before we ask. We can seek His omnipotence, confident that He can intervene in our circumstances. We can rest in His omnipresence, assured that He is always with us. This knowledge enriches our prayer life and deepens our communion with God.

Guided Daily Walk

Recognizing that God's attributes are integral to His essence guides our daily walk with Him. We can live with the assurance of His unchanging presence and promises. We can rely on His wisdom and guidance, knowing that He is all-knowing and all-wise. This understanding shapes our decisions, actions, and attitudes, aligning them with God's character and will.

The Mystery and Majesty of God's Attributes

Despite our efforts to comprehend the full nature of God's attributes, they remain a profound mystery. The finite human mind cannot fully grasp the depth and majesty of the divine. Yet, this mystery invites us into a deeper relationship with God, where faith bridges the gap between understanding and belief.

Isaiah 55:8-9 captures the transcendence of God's ways: "For my thoughts are not your thoughts, neither are your ways my ways, declares the LORD. As the heavens are higher than the earth, so are my ways higher than your ways and my thoughts than your thoughts."

Faith invites us to embrace the mystery of God's attributes, acknowledging our limited understanding while trusting in the revealed truths of scripture. Through faith, we can experience the transformative power of God's character, finding peace, purpose, and direction for our lives.

The attributes of God, such as His omnipotence, omniscience, omnipresence, and immutability, are not merely descriptors but are integral to His very being. Through biblical exegesis, theological reflection, and practical application, we gain a deeper understanding of the profound implications of God's attributes. They are not separate qualities but are fully unified in God's essence.

As we contemplate these truths, may we be inspired to trust in the unchanging, sovereign, and ever-faithful God, whose attributes are a testament to His divine nature. In the words of Psalm 145:3, "Great is the LORD and most worthy of praise; his greatness no one can fathom." This declaration invites us to anchor our faith in the God whose attributes reveal His power, wisdom, presence, and unchanging nature.

Analogies Between the Attributes of God and His Names

The names and attributes of God in the Bible provide profound insights into His nature and character. Both serve as windows through which we can better understand who

God is and how He interacts with His creation. This chapter explores the analogies between the attributes of God and His names, examining how these two aspects of divine revelation complement and reinforce each other. Through biblical exegesis, theological reflection, and practical application, we aim to gain a comprehensive understanding of the interconnectedness between God's names and attributes.

The Significance of God's Names and Attributes

God's names in the Bible are not merely labels but are revelations of His character and essence. Similarly, His attributes describe essential qualities that define His nature. Understanding the analogies between God's names and attributes helps us appreciate the depth of His revelation to humanity.

Biblical Foundations of God's Names and Attributes

The Bible is replete with references to both the names and attributes of God. These references provide a rich tapestry of understanding about who God is and how He relates to His people.

Yahweh (יהוה) and Immutability

One of the most profound names of God is Yahweh, often rendered as Jehovah in English. This name is first revealed in Exodus 3:14-15 when God speaks to Moses from the burning bush:

"God said to Moses, 'I AM WHO I AM. This is what you are to say to the Israelites: I AM has sent me to you.' God also said to Moses, 'Say to the Israelites, "The LORD, the God of your fathers—the God of Abraham, the God of Isaac and the God of Jacob—has sent me to you." This is my name forever, the name you shall call me from generation to generation.'"

Yahweh, derived from the Hebrew verb "to be," signifies God's eternal existence, self-sufficiency, and unchanging nature. This name directly correlates with God's attribute of immutability, which means He does not change. Malachi 3:6 reinforces this attribute: "I the LORD do not change. So you, the descendants of Jacob, are not destroyed."

The name Yahweh encapsulates the essence of God's unchanging nature. Just as God's name Yahweh is constant and enduring, so is His character and His promises. This analogy between the name Yahweh and the attribute of immutability helps us understand that God is reliable and His covenant with His people is steadfast.

El Shaddai (אֵל שַׁדַּי) and Omnipotence

El Shaddai, translated as "God Almighty," emphasizes God's ultimate power and sufficiency. It appears in Genesis 17:1:

"When Abram was ninety-nine years old, the LORD appeared to him and said, 'I am God Almighty; walk before me and be blameless.'"

The name El Shaddai directly correlates with the attribute of omnipotence, which refers to God's all-powerful nature. Revelation 19:6 declares, "For our Lord God Almighty reigns." The term "Almighty" underscores God's supreme power over all things.

El Shaddai reflects God's ability to fulfill His promises and His might in overcoming any obstacle. This name reassures believers of God's power and sovereignty. The analogy between El Shaddai and the attribute of omnipotence helps us understand that God's strength and authority are boundless.

Elohim (אֱלֹהִים) and Sovereignty

Elohim is another significant name used for God, appearing over 2,500 times in the Old Testament. It is a plural noun used singularly to denote the one true God, emphasizing His majesty and power. Genesis 1:1 introduces God as Elohim:

"In the beginning, God created the heavens and the earth."

The name Elohim correlates with the attribute of sovereignty, which signifies God's supreme authority and governance over all creation. Psalm 103:19 states, "The LORD has established his throne in heaven, and his kingdom rules over all."

Elohim as Creator highlights His sovereign power and authority over the universe. This name signifies not just a title but an aspect of God's divine essence. The analogy between Elohim and the attribute of sovereignty helps us recognize God's ultimate control and dominion over all things.

Adonai (אֲדֹנָי) and Lordship

Adonai, meaning "Lord" or "Master," denotes God's authority and lordship. It expresses the relationship between God and His people as one of a master to servants. Isaiah 6:1 depicts a vision of God as Adonai:

"In the year that King Uzziah died, I saw the Lord, high and exalted, seated on a throne; and the train of his robe filled the temple."

The name Adonai correlates with the attribute of lordship, emphasizing God's rightful authority over His creation. Deuteronomy 10:17 highlights this aspect: "For the LORD your God is God of gods and Lord of lords, the great God, mighty and awesome."

Adonai emphasizes God's sovereignty and His role as the master and ruler. This name calls for reverence and submission. The analogy between Adonai and the attribute of lordship helps us understand our relationship with God as one of submission to His divine authority.

Jehovah-Jireh (יְרָאֶה יהוה) and Providence

Jehovah-Jireh, meaning "The Lord Will Provide," is first used in Genesis 22:14, where Abraham names the place where God provided a ram for the sacrifice in place of his son Isaac. "So Abraham called that place The LORD Will Provide. And to this day it is said, 'On the mountain of the LORD it will be provided.'"

This name correlates with the attribute of providence, which refers to God's continuous provision and care for His creation. Philippians 4:19 affirms, "And my God will meet all your needs according to the riches of his glory in Christ Jesus."

Jehovah-Jireh underscores God's provision and care for His people, reassuring believers that God sees their needs and provides for them according to His riches and glory. The analogy between Jehovah-Jireh and the attribute of providence helps us understand God's active involvement in our lives and His ongoing care and provision.

Theological Reflections on the Analogies

The analogies between God's names and attributes provide a deeper understanding of His nature and character.

They reveal that God's names are not mere labels but profound revelations of His divine essence.

Divine Simplicity and Unity

The doctrine of divine simplicity asserts that God is not composed of parts but is entirely unified in His being. This means that God's attributes are not separate components but are fully integrated into His essence. The analogies between God's names and attributes support this doctrine, showing that each name encapsulates aspects of God's nature.

For instance, Yahweh signifies God's unchanging nature, El Shaddai reflects His omnipotence, and Elohim highlights His sovereignty. These names are not separate from God but are integral to who He is. They reveal the unity and coherence of God's nature, ensuring that His attributes are harmoniously integrated into His being.

Assurance of God's Character

Understanding the analogies between God's names and attributes provides assurance of His character. Each name and attribute reveals an aspect of God's nature that is reliable and trustworthy. For example, recognizing God as Yahweh reassures us of His unchanging promises, while understanding Him as El Shaddai comforts us with His boundless power.

These analogies help us trust in God's character, knowing that His names and attributes are consistent and unified. They reinforce our confidence in God's nature and His ability to fulfill His promises.

Practical Implications for Believers

The analogies between God's names and attributes have profound practical implications for believers. They shape our worship, strengthen our faith, and inform our relationship with God.

Deepened Worship

Recognizing the significance of God's names and attributes deepens our worship. Each name invites us to contemplate different aspects of God's character, leading to a more profound reverence and awe. Worshiping God by His names acknowledges His multifaceted nature and honors His divine attributes.

For instance, worshiping God as El Shaddai inspires awe for His omnipotence, while worshiping Him as Jehovah-Jireh fosters gratitude for His provision. These analogies enrich our worship and devotion, drawing us closer to God's heart.

Strengthened Faith

The analogies between God's names and attributes provide a foundation for trust and faith. Understanding that God's names encapsulate His attributes strengthens our confidence in His character. We can rely on God's unchanging nature (Yahweh), His supreme power (El Shaddai), His sovereignty (Elohim), His authority (Adonai), and His provision (Jehovah-Jireh).

These analogies help us trust in God's nature and His ability to fulfill His promises. They reassure us that God's character is reliable and His attributes are integral to His essence.

Informed Relationship

Understanding the analogies between God's names and attributes informs our relationship with Him. Recognizing God's authority as Adonai calls us to submit to His lordship and follow His commands. Understanding Him as Yahweh reassures us of His faithfulness in our daily lives.

These analogies guide our relationship with God, fostering a deeper trust and reliance on His character. They help us align our lives with His nature and purposes, leading to a more intimate and meaningful relationship with Him.

The analogies between the attributes of God and His names provide profound insights into His nature and character. Through biblical exegesis, theological reflection, and practical application, we gain a deeper understanding of the interconnectedness between God's names and attributes. They are not separate components but are fully integrated into His essence, revealing the unity and coherence of His nature.

As we contemplate these analogies, may we be inspired

to trust in the unchanging, sovereign, and ever-faithful God, whose names and attributes are a testament to His divine nature. In the words of Psalm 9:10, "Those who know your name trust in you, for you, LORD, have never forsaken those who seek you." This declaration invites us to anchor our faith in the God who reveals Himself through His many names and attributes, each reflecting His power, authority, and relational nature.

CHAPTER 04

GOD'S AUTHORITY

The authority of God is a fundamental aspect of His divine nature and existence. As the Creator of the heavens and the earth, God possesses absolute authority over all creation. This authority is intrinsic to who God is and is depicted throughout the scriptures, where His sovereign will and commands are paramount. This chapter explores the nature of God's authority, its biblical foundations, and its theological implications, emphasizing how God's authority is inseparable from His very being.

The Nature of God's Authority

God's authority is not derived from any external source; it is inherent in His nature. Unlike human authority, which is often granted or earned, God's authority is intrinsic and absolute. This means that God has the ultimate right and power to govern all that exists. His authority is rooted in His identity as the eternal, self-existent Creator.

God's authority encompasses all aspects of existence, including the physical universe, spiritual realms, and moral order. It is exercised through His sovereign will, which is expressed in His commands, laws, and actions. Understanding God's authority involves recognizing His right to rule and His power to enact His will.

Biblical Foundations of God's Authority

The Bible provides numerous examples of God's authority, beginning with the act of creation. Genesis 1 illustrates how God's authority is exercised through His word.

The Authority of God's Word in Creation

Genesis 1:1-3 states, "In the beginning, God created the heavens and the earth. Now the earth was formless and empty, darkness was over the surface of the deep, and the Spirit of God was hovering over the waters. And God said, 'Let there be light,' and there was light."

This passage highlights the power of God's spoken word. God speaks, and creation responds. The repeated phrase "And God said" throughout Genesis 1 underscores that the universe came into being by God's authoritative command. His word has the power to create, shape, and sustain all things.

Psalm 33:6-9 echoes this theme: "By the word of the LORD the heavens were made, their starry host by the breath of his mouth. He gathers the waters of the sea into jars; he puts the deep into storehouses. Let all the earth fear the LORD; let all the people of the world revere him. For he spoke, and it came to be; he commanded, and it stood firm."

These verses affirm that God's authority is demonstrated through His creative power. His commands are effective and absolute, resulting in the establishment and maintenance of the universe.

The Sovereignty of God

The concept of divine sovereignty is central to understanding God's authority. Sovereignty means that God has supreme power and authority over all creation. This is vividly depicted in passages like Isaiah 45:5-7:

"I am the LORD, and there is no other; apart from me there is no God. I will strengthen you, though you have not acknowledged me, so that from the rising of the sun to the place of its setting people may know there is none besides me. I am the LORD, and there is no other. I form the light and create darkness, I bring prosperity and create disaster; I, the LORD, do all these things."

God's sovereignty is also evident in Daniel 4:34-35, where King Nebuchadnezzar acknowledges God's supreme authority: "His dominion is an eternal dominion; his kingdom endures from generation to generation. All the peoples of the earth are regarded as nothing. He does as he pleases with the powers of heaven and the peoples of the earth. No one can hold back his hand or say to him: 'What have you done?'"

These passages highlight that God's authority is comprehensive and uncontested. He rules over all things with absolute power, and His will is unchallenged.

The Authority of God's Law

God's authority is also expressed through His moral and ethical laws. The Ten Commandments, given to Moses on Mount Sinai, are a direct expression of God's authority over human conduct. Exodus 20:1-3 states:

"And God spoke all these words: 'I am the LORD your God, who brought you out of Egypt, out of the land of slavery. You shall have no other gods before me.'"

God's law reflects His holy and righteous nature. It establishes the moral order for humanity and serves as a guide for righteous living. The authority of God's law is further emphasized in passages like Deuteronomy 6:1-2:

"These are the commands, decrees and laws the LORD your God directed me to teach you to observe in the land that you are crossing the Jordan to possess, so that you, your children and their children after them may fear the LORD your God as long as you live by keeping all his decrees and commands that I give you, and so that you may enjoy long life."

God's authority in giving the law is not merely about rules but about His desire for His people to live in accordance with His will, reflecting His character.

Theological Implications of God's Authority

Understanding God's authority has significant theological implications. It shapes our view of God's nature, our relationship with Him, and our understanding of the world.

God's Nature and Authority

God's authority is inseparable from His other attributes, such as His omnipotence, omniscience, and holiness. His authority is a natural outflow of His all-powerful, all-knowing, and morally perfect nature. Because God is omnipotent, His authority is unchallenged and absolute. Because He is omniscient, His judgments are perfect and just. Because He is holy, His commands are righteous and good.

Human Responsibility and Submission

Recognizing God's authority calls for human submission and obedience. As the Creator and Sustainer of all things, God has the right to command and expect obedience from His creation. James 4:7 exhorts believers: "Submit yourselves, then, to God. Resist the devil, and he will flee from you."

Submission to God's authority involves acknowledging His rightful place as Lord and yielding to His will in all areas of life. This submission is not burdensome but leads to freedom and fulfillment, as it aligns us with the purpose for which we were created.

The Authority of Christ

In the New Testament, the authority of God is also seen in the person of Jesus Christ. Jesus, being fully God, possesses the same authority as the Father. Matthew 28:18 records Jesus' declaration: "All authority in heaven and on earth has been given to me."

Jesus' authority is evident in His teaching, His miracles, and His ability to forgive sins. Mark 1:27 illustrates this: "The people were all so amazed that they asked each other, 'What is this? A new teaching—and with authority! He even gives orders to impure spirits and they obey him.'"

The authority of Christ extends to His role as judge and king, as described in Revelation 19:16: "On his robe and on his thigh he has this name written: KING OF KINGS AND LORD OF LORDS."

Practical Implications for Believers

Understanding and acknowledging God's authority has profound practical implications for believers. It shapes our worship, informs our obedience, and guides our daily lives.

Worship and Reverence

Recognizing God's authority leads to deeper worship and reverence. Acknowledging His supreme power and rightful rule inspires awe and devotion. Psalm 95:6-7 calls us to worship: "Come, let us bow down in worship, let us kneel before the LORD our Maker; for he is our God and we are the people of his pasture, the flock under his care."

Obedience and Submission

Submission to God's authority means living in obedience to His commands. Jesus emphasized this in John 14:15: "If you love me, keep my commands." Obedience is a response to God's authority and an expression of our love and trust in Him.

Trust and Confidence

Knowing that God possesses absolute authority provides comfort and confidence. We can trust that His plans are perfect and His will is good. Romans 8:28 reassures us: "And we know that in all things God works for the good of those who love him, who have been called according to his purpose."

The authority of God is intrinsic to His nature and existence. As the Creator of the heavens and the earth, God possesses absolute authority over all creation. This authority is demonstrated through His word in creation, His sovereign rule, and His righteous law. Understanding God's authority shapes our view of His nature, our relationship with Him, and our understanding of the world.

As we contemplate the authority of God, may we be inspired to trust in His unchanging, sovereign, and ever-faithful nature. In the words of Psalm 103:19, "The LORD has established his throne in heaven, and his kingdom rules over all." This declaration invites us to acknowledge and submit to the supreme authority of God, whose commands are just, whose power is unmatched, and whose will is perfect.

God's Authority in His Governance of the World and His Interaction with Humanity

God's authority is intrinsic to His nature and is demonstrated not only in His act of creation but also in His ongoing governance of the world and His interaction with humanity. He establishes moral laws, delivers judgments, and offers salvation through His covenant relationship with His people. This chapter explores how God's authority manifests in His governance of the world and His relationship with humanity, emphasizing that His authority is inherent and not derived from any external source.

God's Governance of the World

God's authority over the world is evident in His sovereign governance. He upholds the universe, establishes moral order, and executes justice, demonstrating His rule over all creation.

Sustaining the Universe

God's authority is evident in His power to sustain the universe. Hebrews 1:3 states, "The Son is the radiance of God's glory and the exact representation of his being, sustaining all things by his powerful word." This verse highlights that Christ, who shares in God's authority, upholds the universe by His command.

Colossians 1:16-17 further emphasizes this sustaining power: "For in him all things were created: things in heaven and on earth, visible and invisible, whether thrones or powers or rulers or authorities; all things have been created through him and for him. He is before all things, and in him all things hold together."

God's continuous involvement in the world underscores His absolute authority and sovereignty. He maintains the order and existence of the cosmos, ensuring that all creation functions according to His divine plan.

Establishing Moral Order

God's authority is also evident in His establishment of moral laws that govern human conduct. These laws reflect His holy and righteous nature and serve as the foundation for ethical behavior. The Ten Commandments, given to Moses on Mount Sinai, are a prime example of God's moral law.

Exodus 20:1-17 outlines these commandments, beginning with God's authoritative declaration: "I am the LORD your God, who brought you out of Egypt, out of the land of slavery. You shall have no other gods before me."

God's moral laws are not arbitrary rules but expressions of His character. They are designed to guide humanity in living in a manner that reflects His holiness and justice. Deuteronomy 6:1-2 emphasizes the importance of adhering to these laws: "These are the commands, decrees and laws the LORD your God directed me to teach you to observe in the land that you are crossing the Jordan to possess, so that you, your children and their children after them may fear the

LORD your God as long as you live by keeping all his decrees and commands that I give you, and so that you may enjoy long life."

Executing Justice

God's authority includes His role as the ultimate judge who executes justice. His judgments are perfect and righteous, reflecting His omniscience and moral perfection. Psalm 9:7-8 declares, "The LORD reigns forever; he has established his throne for judgment. He rules the world in righteousness and judges the peoples with equity."

Throughout the Bible, God is depicted as the righteous judge who holds individuals and nations accountable for their actions. In the book of Amos, God pronounces judgment on Israel and its neighbors for their injustices and idolatry. Amos 5:24 captures God's desire for justice: "But let justice roll on like a river, righteousness like a never-failing stream!"

God's judgments serve to uphold His moral order and demonstrate His authority over all creation. They remind humanity of the seriousness of sin and the necessity of living in accordance with His commands.

God's Interaction with Humanity

God's authority is also manifest in His interaction with humanity. Through His covenant relationships, His provision of salvation, and His guidance, God engages with His creation in ways that reflect His sovereign authority and love.

Covenant Relationships

Throughout the Bible, God establishes covenant relationships with His people, demonstrating His authority and commitment to them. These covenants are solemn agreements in which God makes promises and sets conditions for His people to follow.

One of the earliest covenants is with Noah, where God promises never to destroy the earth with a flood again. Genesis 9:11 states, "I establish my covenant with you: Never again will all life be destroyed by the waters of a flood; never again will there be a flood to destroy the earth."

The Abrahamic covenant is another significant example, where God promises Abraham descendants, land, and blessing. Genesis 12:2-3 records God's promise: "I will make you into a great nation, and I will bless you; I will make your name great, and you will be a blessing. I will bless those who bless you, and whoever curses you I will curse; and all peoples on earth will be blessed through you."

The Mosaic covenant, given at Mount Sinai, includes the Ten Commandments and other laws that govern Israel's relationship with God. Exodus 19:5-6 emphasizes Israel's role as God's chosen people: "Now if you obey me fully and keep my covenant, then out of all nations you will be my treasured possession. Although the whole earth is mine, you will be for me a kingdom of priests and a holy nation."

Through these covenants, God exercises His authority, setting the terms of His relationship with His people and demonstrating His faithfulness and sovereignty.

Provision of Salvation

God's authority is also evident in His provision of salvation. Throughout the Old and New Testaments, God initiates and accomplishes the redemption of His people, demonstrating His sovereign grace and mercy.

In the Old Testament, God delivers Israel from slavery in Egypt, a powerful act of salvation that establishes His authority over all nations. Exodus 14:13-14 records Moses' words to the Israelites: "Do not be afraid. Stand firm and you will see the deliverance the LORD will bring you today. The Egyptians you see today you will never see again. The LORD will fight for you; you need only to be still."

In the New Testament, God's ultimate act of salvation is through Jesus Christ. John 3:16-17 proclaims, "For God so loved the world that he gave his one and only Son, that whoever believes in him shall not perish but have eternal life. For God did not send his Son into the world to condemn the world, but to save the world through him."

Through Christ's life, death, and resurrection, God offers salvation to all humanity, demonstrating His authority over sin and death. Ephesians 1:7-10 highlights the scope of this redemptive plan: "In him we have redemption through his blood, the forgiveness of sins, in accordance with the riches of God's grace that he lavished on us. With all wisdom and understanding, he made known to us the mystery of his will according to his good pleasure, which he purposed in Christ, to be put into effect when the times reach their fulfillment—to bring unity to all things in heaven and on earth under Christ."

Guidance and Presence

God's authority is also manifest in His guidance and presence with His people. Through the Holy Spirit, God leads, empowers, and comforts believers, demonstrating His ongoing involvement in their lives.

In the Old Testament, God's presence is symbolized by the Ark of the Covenant and the Tabernacle, where He dwells among His people. Exodus 25:8-9 states, "Then have them make a sanctuary for me, and I will dwell among them. Make this tabernacle and all its furnishings exactly like the pattern I will show you."

In the New Testament, Jesus promises the Holy Spirit to His disciples, ensuring God's continual presence and guidance. John 14:16-17 records Jesus' promise: "And I will ask the Father, and he will give you another advocate to help you and be with you forever—the Spirit of truth. The world cannot accept him, because it neither sees him nor knows him. But you know him, for he lives with you and will be in you."

The Holy Spirit empowers believers to live according to God's will, providing wisdom, strength, and comfort. Galatians 5:22-23 describes the fruit of the Spirit: "But the fruit of the Spirit is love, joy, peace, forbearance, kindness, goodness, faithfulness, gentleness and self-control. Against such things there is no law."

Theological Implications of God's Authority

Understanding God's authority in His governance of the world and His interaction with humanity has significant theological implications. It shapes our view of God's nature, our relationship with Him, and our understanding of salvation.

God's Nature and Authority

God's authority is integral to His nature. It reflects His omnipotence, omniscience, and moral perfection. God's governance of the world and His interaction with humanity demonstrate His sovereign power, wisdom, and love.

Recognizing God's authority helps us appreciate the depth of His character and the extent of His involvement in our lives.

Human Responsibility and Submission

Acknowledging God's authority calls for human responsibility and submission. As the Creator and Sustainer of all things, God has the right to command and expect obedience from His creation. James 4:7 exhorts believers: "Submit yourselves, then, to God. Resist the devil, and he will flee from you."

Submission to God's authority involves recognizing His rightful place as Lord and yielding to His will in all areas of life. This submission leads to freedom and fulfillment, aligning us with the purpose for which we were created.

Assurance of Salvation

Understanding God's authority in providing salvation offers assurance to believers. Salvation is not based on human effort but on God's sovereign grace and mercy. Ephesians 2:8-9 emphasizes this: "For it is by grace you have been saved, through faith—and this is not from yourselves, it is the gift of God—not by works, so that no one can boast."

God's authority ensures the security of our salvation. Romans 8:38-39 provides a powerful reminder of this assurance: "For I am convinced that neither death nor life, neither angels nor demons, neither the present nor the future, nor any powers, neither height nor depth, nor anything else in all creation, will be able to separate us from the love of God that is in Christ Jesus our Lord."

Practical Implications for Believers

Understanding and acknowledging God's authority in His governance of the world and His interaction with humanity has profound practical implications for believers. It shapes our worship, informs our obedience, and guides our daily lives.

Worship and Reverence

Recognizing God's authority leads to deeper worship and reverence. Acknowledging His supreme power and rightful rule inspires awe and devotion. Psalm 95:6-7 calls us to worship: "Come, let us bow down in worship, let us kneel before the LORD our Maker; for he is our God and we are the people of his pasture, the flock under his care."

Obedience and Submission

Submission to God's authority means living in obedience to His commands. Jesus emphasized this in John 14:15: "If you love me, keep my commands." Obedience is a response to God's authority and an expression of our love and trust in Him.

Trust and Confidence

Knowing that God possesses absolute authority provides comfort and confidence. We can trust that His plans are perfect and His will is good. Romans 8:28 reassures us: "And we know that in all things God works for the good of those who love him, who have been called according to his purpose."

God's authority in His governance of the world and His interaction with humanity is intrinsic to His nature and existence. As the Creator and Sustainer of all things, God possesses absolute authority over all creation. This authority is demonstrated through His sustaining power, His moral laws, His judgments, and His provision of salvation. Understanding God's authority shapes our view of His nature, our relationship with Him, and our understanding of the world.

As we contemplate God's authority, may we be inspired to trust in His unchanging, sovereign, and ever-faithful nature. In the words of Psalm 103:19, "The LORD has established his throne in heaven, and his kingdom rules over all." This declaration invites us to acknowledge and submit to the supreme authority of God, whose commands are just, whose power is unmatched, and whose will is perfect.

The Theological Significance of God's Intrinsic Omnipotence

God's omnipotence, His all-encompassing power, is a fundamental attribute that defines His nature and character. This intrinsic omnipotence means that God's power is inherent and absolute, not derived from any external source. Understanding God's omnipotence is crucial for comprehending His authority, sovereignty, and the way He interacts with creation. This chapter explores the theological significance of God's intrinsic omnipotence, examining its biblical foundations, implications for theology, and practical relevance for believers.

Biblical Foundations of God's Omnipotence

The Bible provides numerous references to God's omnipotence, portraying Him as the Almighty Creator and Sustainer of the universe. These passages highlight the extent and nature of God's power.

Omnipotence in Creation

God's omnipotence is first demonstrated in the act of creation. Genesis 1:1 states, "In the beginning, God created the heavens and the earth." The power of God's word is further emphasized in Genesis 1:3: "And God said, 'Let there be light,' and there was light." This creative act reveals that God's power is unlimited and effective.

Psalm 33:6-9 reiterates God's creative omnipotence: "By the word of the LORD the heavens were made, their starry host by the breath of his mouth. ... For he spoke, and it came to be; he commanded, and it stood firm." These verses underscore that God's spoken word is powerful enough to bring the universe into existence.

Omnipotence in Sustaining Creation

God's omnipotence is not limited to creation but extends to sustaining the universe. Colossians 1:16-17 states, "For in him all things were created: things in heaven and on earth, visible and invisible, whether thrones or powers or rulers or authorities; all things have been created through him and for him. He is before all things, and in him all things hold together." This passage highlights that God's power upholds and maintains all creation.

Hebrews 1:3 also affirms this sustaining power: "The Son is the radiance of God's glory and the exact representation of his being, sustaining all things by his powerful word." Jesus Christ, as the embodiment of God's omnipotence, continually sustains the universe.

Omnipotence in Salvation and Judgment

God's omnipotence is evident in His ability to save and judge. Isaiah 40:28-31 portrays God's power to strengthen and renew His people: "Do you not know? Have you not heard? The LORD is the everlasting God, the Creator of the ends of the earth. He will not grow tired or weary, and his understanding no one can fathom. He gives strength to the weary and increases the power of the weak."

God's power to judge is emphasized in passages like Revelation 19:15: "Coming out of his mouth is a sharp sword with which to strike down the nations. 'He will rule them with an iron scepter.' He treads the winepress of the fury of the wrath of God Almighty." This verse highlights God's authority and power to execute judgment.

Theological Implications of God's Intrinsic Omnipotence

Understanding God's intrinsic omnipotence has profound theological implications. It shapes our understanding of His nature, His relationship with creation, and the way we approach Him in faith and worship.

The Nature of God

God's intrinsic omnipotence is a fundamental aspect of His nature. It means that God's power is not dependent on anything outside of Himself. He possesses infinite power inherently, and His omnipotence is a defining attribute of His being. This intrinsic power sets God apart from all creation, underscoring His uniqueness and divinity.

Sovereignty and Authority

God's omnipotence is directly related to His sovereignty and authority. Because God is all-powerful, He has the ultimate authority over all creation. His will is supreme, and nothing can thwart His purposes. Daniel 4:35 captures this reality: "All the peoples of the earth are regarded as nothing. He does as he pleases with the powers of heaven and the peoples of the earth. No one can hold back his hand or say to him: 'What have you done?'"

This sovereignty assures believers that God is in control, regardless of circumstances. It provides comfort and confidence that God's plans will prevail, and His purposes will be accomplished.

The Reliability of God's Promises

God's omnipotence guarantees the reliability of His promises. Because God is all-powerful, He can fulfill every promise He makes. Isaiah 55:10-11 illustrates this: "As the rain and the snow come down from heaven, and do not return to it without watering the earth and making it bud and flourish, so that it yields seed for the sower and bread for the eater, so is my word that goes out from my mouth: It will not return to me empty, but will accomplish what I desire and achieve the purpose for which I sent it."

Believers can trust in God's promises, knowing that His omnipotence ensures their fulfillment. This trust fosters faith and hope, providing assurance in God's faithfulness.

Relationship with Creation

God's omnipotence shapes His relationship with creation. As the all-powerful Creator and Sustainer, God is intimately involved in the workings of the universe. His power is not distant or detached but actively upholds and governs all things. This involvement is reflected in passages like Acts 17:28: "For in him we live and move and have our being."

God's omnipotence also implies His care and provision for creation. Jesus highlights this in Matthew 6:26: "Look at the birds of the air; they do not sow or reap or store away in barns, and yet your heavenly Father feeds them. Are you not much more valuable than they?" God's power ensures that all creation is sustained and provided for.

Practical Implications for Believers

Understanding God's intrinsic omnipotence has significant practical implications for believers. It shapes our worship, informs our prayers, and guides our daily lives.

Worship and Reverence

Recognizing God's omnipotence deepens our worship and reverence. Acknowledging His supreme power inspires awe and adoration. Psalm 145:3 declares, "Great is the LORD and most worthy of praise; his greatness no one can fathom." Worshiping God for His omnipotence honors His majesty and acknowledges His infinite power.

Trust and Confidence

God's omnipotence provides a foundation for trust and confidence. Believers can rely on God's power to sustain them through all circumstances. Psalm 46:1-2 reassures us, "God is our refuge and strength, an ever-present help in trouble. Therefore we will not fear, though the earth give way and the mountains fall into the heart of the sea."

This trust in God's power fosters peace and stability, even in the midst of trials and uncertainties. It encourages believers to depend on God's strength rather than their own abilities.

Prayer and Petition

Understanding God's omnipotence informs our prayers and petitions. Knowing that God has the power to answer prayers gives confidence in approaching Him with our needs and requests. Ephesians 3:20-21 emphasizes God's ability to do more than we can imagine: "Now to him who is able to do immeasurably more than all we ask or imagine, according to his power that is at work within us, to him be glory in the church and in Christ Jesus throughout all generations, for ever and ever! Amen."

This understanding encourages believers to pray boldly and expectantly, trusting in God's power to act on their behalf.

Obedience and Submission

God's omnipotence calls for obedience and submission. Recognizing His supreme power and authority compels believers to submit to His will and follow His commands. James 4:7 exhorts, "Submit yourselves, then, to God. Resist the devil, and he will flee from you."

Submission to God's omnipotence aligns our lives with His purposes and leads to spiritual growth and fulfillment. It involves yielding our desires and plans to God's sovereign will, trusting that His power will accomplish what is best for us.

The Mystery and Majesty of God's Omnipotence

Despite our efforts to understand God's omnipotence, it remains a profound mystery. The finite human mind cannot fully grasp the extent of God's infinite power. Yet, this mystery invites us into a deeper relationship with God, where faith bridges the gap between understanding and belief.

Isaiah 40:28-31 captures the transcendence of God's power: "Do you not know? Have you not heard? The LORD is the everlasting God, the Creator of the ends of the earth. He will not grow tired or weary, and his understanding no one can fathom. He gives strength to the weary and increases the power of the weak."

Faith invites us to embrace the mystery of God's omnipotence, acknowledging our limited understanding while trusting in the revealed truths of scripture. Through faith, we can experience the transformative power of God's omnipotence, finding peace, purpose, and direction for our lives.

God's intrinsic omnipotence is a fundamental aspect of His divine nature. It is demonstrated in His creation and sustenance of the universe, His ability to save and judge, and His ongoing involvement in the world. Understanding God's omnipotence shapes our view of His nature, our relationship with Him, and our understanding of His promises.

As we contemplate God's omnipotence, may we be inspired to trust in His unchanging, sovereign, and ever-faithful nature. In the words of Jeremiah 32:17, "Ah, Sovereign LORD, you have made the heavens and the earth by your great power and outstretched arm. Nothing is too hard for you." This declaration invites us to acknowledge and submit to the supreme power of God, whose omnipotence ensures the fulfillment of His promises and the accomplishment of His will.

CHAPTER 05

UNDERSTANDING THE INFINITE

The infinite nature of God is a profound and often perplexing concept that challenges the limits of human understanding. Our finite minds, shaped by temporal experiences and limited perceptions, struggle to fully grasp the notions of eternity, self-existence, and absolute authority. Yet, despite these limitations, faith invites us to trust in the truths revealed in scripture and to seek a deeper relationship with God. This chapter delves into the human struggle to comprehend the infinite nature of God and explores how faith bridges the gap between our finite understanding and divine mystery.

The Limitations of Human Understanding

Human beings are inherently finite. Our lives are bound by time, space, and the physical world, shaping our perceptions and understanding. Concepts such as infinity, eternity, and absolute authority often lie beyond our experiential realm, making them difficult to fully comprehend.

Finite Minds and Infinite Concepts

The finite nature of human minds means that we are accustomed to beginnings and endings, measurable quantities, and limited capacities. When faced with the idea of God's infinite nature, which encompasses endless existence, boundless power, and limitless knowledge, our cognitive frameworks fall short.

Isaiah 55:8-9 captures this disparity: "For my thoughts are not your thoughts, neither are your ways my ways," declares the LORD. "As the heavens are higher than the earth, so are my ways higher than your ways and my thoughts than your thoughts." This passage highlights the vast difference between God's infinite nature and human understanding.

The Challenge of Comprehending Eternity

Eternity, the concept of endless time, is particularly challenging for finite beings to grasp. We live within the constraints of linear time, marked by past, present, and future.

The idea that God exists outside of time, having no beginning or end, stretches our imagination.

Psalm 90:2 emphasizes God's eternal nature: "Before the mountains were born or you brought forth the whole world, from everlasting to everlasting you are God." This eternal existence is fundamentally different from our temporal experience, making it a difficult concept to fully internalize.

The Mystery of Self-Existence

God's self-existence, or aseity, is another concept that challenges human understanding. Unlike all created beings who derive their existence from something else, God exists by His own power and will. This self-sufficiency is a core attribute of His divine nature.

In Exodus 3:14, God reveals His self-existence to Moses: "God said to Moses, 'I AM WHO I AM. This is what you are to say to the Israelites: I AM has sent me to you.'" The name "I AM" signifies that God is the ground of His own being, a reality that is fundamentally different from the contingent nature of human existence.

Absolute Authority and Sovereignty

God's absolute authority and sovereignty over all creation is another aspect of His infinite nature that challenges human comprehension. We are accustomed to authority structures that are limited and derived from external sources. In contrast, God's authority is intrinsic and unlimited.

Daniel 4:35 describes God's sovereign authority: "All the peoples of the earth are regarded as nothing. He does as he pleases with the powers of heaven and the peoples of the earth. No one can hold back his hand or say to him: 'What have you done?'" This absolute sovereignty highlights the vast difference between God's authority and human experience.

Faith and the Infinite

Despite the limitations of human understanding, faith provides a means to engage with the infinite nature of God. Faith invites us to trust in the truths revealed in scripture, even when they transcend our cognitive capacities.

Trusting in Divine Revelation

Scripture reveals aspects of God's infinite nature that we are called to trust, even when we cannot fully understand them. Hebrews 11:1 defines faith as "confidence in what we hope for and assurance about what we do not see." Faith involves trusting in God's self-revelation, knowing that His infinite nature is beyond our full comprehension.

Faith accepts the mystery of God's nature, acknowledging that His thoughts and ways are higher than ours. It allows us to rest in the assurance that God is who He says He is, even when our understanding is limited.

Embracing the Mystery

Faith encourages us to embrace the mystery of God's infinite nature, recognizing that some aspects of His being are beyond human understanding. Deuteronomy 29:29 reminds us, "The secret things belong to the LORD our God, but the things revealed belong to us and to our children forever, that we may follow all the words of this law."

This verse acknowledges that while some things about God remain hidden, He has revealed enough for us to know and follow Him. Embracing the mystery of God's nature leads us to a posture of humility and awe, fostering a deeper reverence for Him.

Seeking a Deeper Relationship

Faith not only bridges the gap between our finite understanding and God's infinite nature but also invites us into a deeper relationship with Him. Through prayer, worship, and study of scripture, we can grow in our knowledge and love of God.

Jeremiah 29:13 promises, "You will seek me and find me when you seek me with all your heart." This invitation encourages believers to pursue a deeper understanding of God, knowing that He desires to reveal Himself to those who earnestly seek Him.

Practical Implications for Believers

Understanding the struggle to comprehend God's infinite nature has practical implications for believers. It shapes our approach to theology, worship, and daily life.

Approach to Theology

Recognizing the limitations of human understanding encourages a humble approach to theology. It reminds us that our knowledge of God is always partial and that we must rely on divine revelation and the guidance of the Holy Spirit.

1 Corinthians 13:12 reflects this humility: "For now we see only a reflection as in a mirror; then we shall see face to face. Now I know in part; then I shall know fully, even as I am fully known." This verse acknowledges the partial nature of our current understanding and the promise of fuller knowledge in the future.

Worship and Reverence

The awareness of God's infinite nature deepens our worship and reverence. Recognizing the vastness of God's being inspires awe and adoration, leading us to worship Him with greater fervor.

Psalm 145:3 captures this sentiment: "Great is the LORD and most worthy of praise; his greatness no one can fathom." Worshiping God for His infinite attributes honors His majesty and acknowledges His incomprehensible nature.

Daily Life and Trust

Understanding the struggle to comprehend God's infinite nature encourages trust and dependence on Him in daily life. It reminds us that while we may not understand everything about God, we can trust in His character and His promises.

Proverbs 3:5-6 advises, "Trust in the LORD with all your heart and lean not on your own understanding; in all your ways submit to him, and he will make your paths straight." This trust leads to a life of faith, relying on God's wisdom and guidance.

The human struggle to comprehend the infinite nature of God highlights the limitations of our finite understanding. Concepts such as eternity, self-existence, and absolute authority challenge our cognitive capacities, yet faith bridges the gap between our limited understanding and divine mystery.

As we trust in the truths revealed in scripture, embrace the mystery of God's nature, and seek a deeper relationship with Him, we can grow in our knowledge and love of the infinite God. In the words of Ephesians 3:17-19, "And I pray that you, being rooted and established in love, may have power, together with all the Lord's holy people, to grasp how wide and long and high and deep is the love of Christ, and to know this love that surpasses knowledge—that you may be filled to the measure of all the fullness of God."

This prayer invites us to seek a deeper understanding of God's infinite nature, knowing that His love and being surpass all knowledge. Through faith, we can engage with the divine mystery and experience the transformative power of God's infinite nature in our lives.

The Infinite Nature of God

Isaiah 55:8-9 captures a profound truth about the nature of God: "For my thoughts are not your thoughts, neither are your ways my ways," declares the LORD. "As the heavens are higher than the earth, so are my ways higher than your ways and my thoughts than your thoughts." This passage reminds us that God's nature and ways are beyond our full comprehension. While our finite minds struggle to grasp concepts such as eternity, self-existence, and absolute authority, faith invites us to trust in God's wisdom and sovereignty. This chapter explores the human struggle to comprehend the infinite nature of God and how faith bridges the gap between our limited understanding and divine mystery.

The Limitations of Human Understanding

Human beings are inherently finite. Our lives are bound by time, space, and the physical world, shaping our perceptions and understanding. Concepts such as infinity, eternity, and absolute authority often lie beyond our experiential realm, making them difficult to fully comprehend.

Finite Minds and Infinite Concepts

Our finite nature means we are accustomed to beginnings and endings, measurable quantities, and limited capacities. When faced with the idea of God's infinite nature—encompassing endless existence, boundless power, and limitless knowledge—our cognitive frameworks fall short. Isaiah 55:8-9 highlights this disparity: God's thoughts and ways are infinitely higher than ours, emphasizing the vast difference between the divine and the human.

The Challenge of Comprehending Eternity

Eternity, the concept of endless time, is particularly challenging for finite beings to grasp. We live within the constraints of linear time, marked by past, present, and future. The idea that God exists outside of time, having no beginning or end, stretches our imagination. Psalm 90:2 emphasizes God's eternal nature: "Before the mountains were born or you brought forth the whole world, from everlasting to everlasting you are God." This eternal existence is fundamentally different from our temporal experience, making it a difficult concept to fully internalize.

The Mystery of Self-Existence

God's self-existence, or aseity, is another concept that challenges human understanding. Unlike all created beings who derive their existence from something else, God exists by His own power and will. This self-sufficiency is a core attribute of His divine nature. In Exodus 3:14, God reveals His self-existence to Moses: "God said to Moses, 'I AM WHO I AM. This is what you are to say to the Israelites: I AM has sent me to you.'" The name "I AM" signifies that God is the ground of His own being, a reality fundamentally different from the contingent nature of human existence.

Absolute Authority and Sovereignty

God's absolute authority and sovereignty over all creation is another aspect of His infinite nature that challenges human comprehension. We are accustomed to authority structures that are limited and derived from external sources. In contrast, God's authority is intrinsic and unlimited. Daniel 4:35 describes God's sovereign authority: "All the peoples of the earth are regarded as nothing. He does as he pleases with the powers of heaven and the peoples of the earth. No one can hold back his hand or say to him: 'What have you done?'" This absolute sovereignty highlights the vast difference between God's authority and human experience.

Faith and the Infinite

Despite the limitations of human understanding, faith provides a means to engage with the infinite nature of God. Faith invites us to trust in the truths revealed in scripture, even when they transcend our cognitive capacities.

Trusting in Divine Revelation

Scripture reveals aspects of God's infinite nature that we are called to trust, even when we cannot fully understand them. Hebrews 11:1 defines faith as "confidence in what we hope for and assurance about what we do not see." Faith involves trusting in God's self-revelation, knowing that His infinite nature is beyond our full comprehension. Faith accepts the mystery of God's nature, acknowledging that His thoughts and ways are higher than ours. It allows us to rest in the assurance that God is who He says He is, even when our understanding is limited.

Embracing the Mystery

Faith encourages us to embrace the mystery of God's infinite nature, recognizing that some aspects of His being are beyond human understanding. Deuteronomy 29:29 reminds us, "The secret things belong to the LORD our God, but the things revealed belong to us and to our children forever, that we may follow all the words of this law." This verse acknowledges that while some things about God remain hidden, He has revealed enough for us to know and follow

Him. Embracing the mystery of God's nature leads us to a posture of humility and awe, fostering a deeper reverence for Him.

Seeking a Deeper Relationship

Faith not only bridges the gap between our finite understanding and God's infinite nature but also invites us into a deeper relationship with Him. Through prayer, worship, and the study of scripture, we can grow in our knowledge and love of God. Jeremiah 29:13 promises, "You will seek me and find me when you seek me with all your heart." This invitation encourages believers to pursue a deeper understanding of God, knowing that He desires to reveal Himself to those who earnestly seek Him.

Practical Implications for Believers

Understanding the struggle to comprehend God's infinite nature has practical implications for believers. It shapes our approach to theology, worship, and daily life.

Approach to Theology

Recognizing the limitations of human understanding encourages a humble approach to theology. It reminds us that our knowledge of God is always partial and that we must rely on divine revelation and the guidance of the Holy Spirit. 1 Corinthians 13:12 reflects this humility: "For now we see only a reflection as in a mirror; then we shall see face to face. Now

I know in part; then I shall know fully, even as I am fully known." This verse acknowledges the partial nature of our current understanding and the promise of fuller knowledge in the future.

Worship and Reverence

The awareness of God's infinite nature deepens our worship and reverence. Recognizing the vastness of God's being inspires awe and adoration, leading us to worship Him with greater fervor. Psalm 145:3 captures this sentiment: "Great is the LORD and most worthy of praise; his greatness no one can fathom." Worshiping God for His infinite attributes honors His majesty and acknowledges His incomprehensible nature.

Daily Life and Trust

Understanding the struggle to comprehend God's infinite nature encourages trust and dependence on Him in daily life. It reminds us that while we may not understand everything about God, we can trust in His character and His promises. Proverbs 3:5-6 advises, "Trust in the LORD with all your heart and lean not on your own understanding; in all your ways submit to him, and he will make your paths straight." This trust leads to a life of faith, relying on God's wisdom and guidance.

The human struggle to comprehend the infinite nature of God highlights the limitations of our finite understanding. Concepts such as eternity, self-existence, and absolute authority challenge our cognitive capacities, yet faith bridges the gap between our limited understanding and divine mystery.

As we trust in the truths revealed in scripture, embrace the mystery of God's nature, and seek a deeper relationship with Him, we can grow in our knowledge and love of the infinite God. In the words of Ephesians 3:17-19, "And I pray that you, being rooted and established in love, may have power, together with all the Lord's holy people, to grasp how wide and long and high and deep is the love of Christ, and to know this love that surpasses knowledge—that you may be filled to the measure of all the fullness of God."

This prayer invites us to seek a deeper understanding of God's infinite nature, knowing that His love and being surpass all knowledge. Through faith, we can engage with the divine mystery and experience the transformative power of God's infinite nature in our lives.

Understanding God's Eternal Nature through Mathematical Infinity

The concept of infinity in mathematics offers a compelling analogy for understanding the eternal nature of

God. Infinity, denoted by the symbol ∞, represents something that is unbounded or limitless. When applied to the nature of God, it helps illustrate the idea that God is eternal—having no beginning and no end. This chapter explores how the mathematical concept of infinity can deepen our understanding of God's eternal nature, particularly in the context of the Trinity: the Father, the Word (Jesus), and the Holy Spirit.

The Concept of Infinity

In mathematics, infinity is not a number but a concept that describes something without any limit. Infinity cannot be quantified or measured; it goes beyond the constraints of finite understanding. The properties of infinity can be summed up in equations like $\infty + \infty + \infty = \infty$, demonstrating that adding infinite quantities still results in infinity. This characteristic mirrors the eternal nature of God, who exists beyond the bounds of time and space.

The Eternal Nature of God

The Bible consistently describes God as eternal, emphasizing His existence without beginning or end. This eternal nature is inherent in each person of the Trinity: the Father, the Son (Jesus), and the Holy Spirit.

The Father: Eternal and Infinite

The Father is described as eternal in numerous scriptures. Psalm 90:2 declares, "Before the mountains were born or you brought forth the whole world, from everlasting to everlasting you are God." This verse highlights the Father's eternal existence, spanning beyond any temporal limits.

The Father's eternity can be understood through the lens of infinity. Just as infinity has no starting or ending point, the Father exists eternally, beyond the confines of time. His eternal nature signifies an unchanging, ever-present reality that transcends our finite comprehension.

The Word (Jesus): Eternal and Infinite

The Word, Jesus Christ, is also described as eternal. John 1:1-2 states, "In the beginning was the Word, and the Word was with God, and the Word was God. He was with God in the beginning." This passage underscores that Jesus, the Word, existed eternally with God before the creation of the world.

Jesus Himself affirms His eternal nature in Revelation 22:13: "I am the Alpha and the Omega, the First and the Last, the Beginning and the End." These titles signify Jesus' existence beyond time's constraints, mirroring the infinite nature of God. Just as infinity encompasses all numbers without limitation, Jesus' existence spans all of time, from eternity past to eternity future.

The Holy Spirit: Eternal and Infinite

The Holy Spirit is also eternal. Hebrews 9:14 refers to "the eternal Spirit," highlighting the Holy Spirit's everlasting nature. The Spirit's work and presence are not confined to temporal limits but extend infinitely.

The Holy Spirit's eternity can be understood through the same analogy of infinity. Just as infinity is boundless, the Holy Spirit exists and operates beyond the limits of time and space, continually active and present throughout all of creation and history.

The Trinity: Three Are One

The doctrine of the Trinity states that the Father, the Son (Jesus), and the Holy Spirit are three distinct persons but one God. This concept is expressed in 1 John 5:7: "For there are three that bear witness in heaven: the Father, the Word, and the Holy Spirit; and these three are one."

Mathematical Analogy of Infinity and the Trinity

The mathematical analogy of infinity helps us understand the unity and distinction within the Trinity. Just as $\infty + \infty + \infty = \infty$, the three persons of the Trinity, each infinite and eternal, are one God. This equation illustrates that the addition of infinite quantities still results in infinity, symbolizing the unity of the three persons in one divine essence.

The Father, Son, and Holy Spirit, though distinct, share the same infinite nature and essence. Their eternal existence and infinite attributes are not divided or diminished but perfectly unified in the Godhead.

Theological Implications of God's Eternal Nature

Understanding God's eternal nature through the concept of infinity has profound theological implications. It shapes our understanding of God's character, His relationship with creation, and His work in salvation.

God's Unchanging Nature

God's eternal nature signifies His immutability—His unchanging character. Hebrews 13:8 states, "Jesus Christ is the same yesterday and today and forever." This assurance of God's constancy provides stability and confidence for believers, knowing that God's nature and promises are steadfast.

God's Sovereignty and Omnipresence

God's eternity underscores His sovereignty and omnipresence. As an infinite being, God exists everywhere and at all times. Psalm 139:7-10 captures this truth: "Where can I go from your Spirit? Where can I flee from your presence? If I go up to the heavens, you are there; if I make my bed in the depths, you are there. If I rise on the wings of the dawn, if I settle on the far side of the sea, even there your hand will guide me, your right hand will hold me fast."

God's infinite presence assures believers of His continual guidance and support, regardless of circumstances.

The Eternal Plan of Salvation

God's eternal nature also relates to His eternal plan of salvation. Ephesians 1:4-5 reveals that God's plan of salvation through Jesus Christ was established "before the creation of the world." This eternal plan reflects God's infinite wisdom and love, demonstrating His unchanging commitment to redeem humanity.

The eternal nature of the Trinity plays a crucial role in the work of salvation. The Father sends the Son to redeem the world, and the Holy Spirit applies the work of redemption to believers' lives. This collaborative work of the Trinity, grounded in their eternal and infinite nature, ensures the efficacy and permanence of salvation.

Practical Implications for Believers

Understanding God's eternal and infinite nature has significant practical implications for believers. It shapes our worship, trust, and perspective on life and eternity.

Worship and Reverence

Recognizing the infinite nature of God deepens our worship and reverence. Acknowledging His eternal existence and limitless attributes inspires awe and adoration. Psalm 145:3 declares, "Great is the LORD and most worthy of praise; his greatness no one can fathom." Worshiping God for His infinite nature honors His majesty and acknowledges His incomprehensible greatness.

Trust and Confidence

God's eternal and infinite nature provides a foundation for trust and confidence. Believers can rely on God's unchanging character and eternal promises. Isaiah 40:28-31 reassures us: "Do you not know? Have you not heard? The LORD is the everlasting God, the Creator of the ends of the earth. He will not grow tired or weary, and his understanding no one can fathom. He gives strength to the weary and increases the power of the weak."

This trust in God's infinite power and wisdom fosters peace and stability, even in the midst of life's uncertainties.

Perspective on Life and Eternity

Understanding God's eternal nature shapes our perspective on life and eternity. It reminds us that our lives are part of a larger, eternal plan. 2 Corinthians 4:17-18 encourages believers: "For our light and momentary troubles are achieving for us an eternal glory that far outweighs them all. So we fix our eyes not on what is seen, but on what is unseen, since what is seen is temporary, but what is unseen is eternal."

This eternal perspective helps us prioritize what truly matters and live with a focus on God's eternal purposes.

The concept of infinity in mathematics provides a meaningful analogy for understanding the eternal nature of God. The Father, the Word (Jesus), and the Holy Spirit each possess an infinite and eternal nature, reflecting the unity and distinction within the Trinity. This understanding shapes our view of God's character, His relationship with creation, and His work in salvation.

As we contemplate the infinite nature of God, may we be inspired to trust in His unchanging, sovereign, and ever-faithful nature. In the words of 1 John 5:7, "For there are three that bear witness in heaven: the Father, the Word, and the Holy Spirit; and these three are one." This declaration invites us to acknowledge and worship the eternal God, whose infinite nature surpasses all understanding and whose love and presence endure forever.

CHAPTER 06

THE POWER OF THE EVERLASTING GOD

Believing in the everlasting nature of God has profound implications for our lives. It means trusting in a God who is unchanging, reliable, and eternally present. This belief offers comfort and assurance, especially in times of uncertainty and difficulty. The power of the everlasting God can change our stories, offering hope, transformation, and salvation through Jesus Christ. This chapter explores how the everlasting nature of God impacts our lives, providing a source of strength and inspiration.

The Everlasting Nature of God

God's everlasting nature is a fundamental aspect of His character. He exists outside of time, with no beginning or end. This eternal existence sets God apart from all creation and underscores His immutability and faithfulness.

Scriptural Foundations

The Bible provides numerous references to God's everlasting nature. Psalm 90:2 declares, "Before the mountains were born or you brought forth the whole world, from everlasting to everlasting you are God." This verse emphasizes that God's existence transcends time and space.

Isaiah 40:28 also highlights God's eternal nature: "Do you not know? Have you not heard? The LORD is the everlasting God, the Creator of the ends of the earth. He will not grow tired or weary, and his understanding no one can fathom." This passage reassures us that God's strength and wisdom are infinite and unchanging.

The Implications of God's Everlasting Nature

God's everlasting nature implies several key attributes that are essential for understanding His character and His relationship with us:

1. Immutability: God does not change. Malachi 3:6 states, "I the LORD do not change. So you, the descendants of Jacob, are not destroyed." This immutability assures us that God's promises and character remain constant.

2. Faithfulness: God's eternal nature underscores His faithfulness. Lamentations 3:22-23 affirms, "Because of the

LORD's great love we are not consumed, for his compassions never fail. They are new every morning; great is your faithfulness."

3. Omnipresence: God's everlasting nature means He is always present. Psalm 139:7-10 reflects this truth: "Where can I go from your Spirit? Where can I flee from your presence? ... even there your hand will guide me, your right hand will hold me fast."

The Power of the Everlasting God in Our Lives

Believing in the everlasting nature of God transforms how we live and view the world. It offers us hope, strength, and assurance in every aspect of our lives.

Comfort in Times of Uncertainty

In a world filled with uncertainty and change, the everlasting nature of God provides a stable foundation. Knowing that God is unchanging and eternally present gives us peace and confidence. Hebrews 13:8 reminds us, "Jesus Christ is the same yesterday and today and forever."

This assurance is particularly comforting during times of crisis and difficulty. Psalm 46:1-2 declares, "God is our refuge and strength, an ever-present help in trouble. Therefore we will not fear, though the earth give way and the mountains fall into the heart of the sea." Trusting in the everlasting God means that we have a constant source of help and comfort, no matter what challenges we face.

Hope for Transformation

The power of the everlasting God brings hope for transformation. God's eternal nature means that His power to change lives is limitless. 2 Corinthians 5:17 proclaims, "Therefore, if anyone is in Christ, the new creation has come: The old has gone, the new is here!"

This transformative power is available to all who believe in Jesus Christ. God's ability to renew and restore is not bound by time or circumstance. Philippians 1:6 assures us, "being confident of this, that he who began a good work in you will carry it on to completion until the day of Christ Jesus." Our faith in the everlasting God gives us hope that we can experience continual growth and renewal.

Assurance of Salvation

Believing in the everlasting nature of God also gives us assurance of salvation. God's eternal promises and His unchanging nature mean that our salvation is secure in Him. John 10:28-29 provides this assurance: "I give them eternal life, and they shall never perish; no one will snatch them out of my hand. My Father, who has given them to me, is greater than all; no one can snatch them out of my Father's hand."

This security is grounded in the unchanging character of God. Romans 8:38-39 emphasizes that nothing can separate us from God's love: "For I am convinced that neither death nor life, neither angels nor demons, neither the present nor the future, nor any powers, neither height nor depth, nor anything else in all creation, will be able to separate us from the love of God that is in Christ Jesus our Lord."

Practical Implications of Believing in an Everlasting God

Believing in the everlasting nature of God has practical implications for how we live our daily lives. It influences our priorities, our relationships, and our approach to challenges.

Prioritizing Eternal Values

Understanding God's everlasting nature encourages us to prioritize eternal values over temporal concerns. Jesus teaches this in Matthew 6:19-21: "Do not store up for yourselves treasures on earth, where moths and vermin destroy, and where thieves break in and steal. But store up for yourselves treasures in heaven, where moths and vermin do not destroy, and where thieves do not break in and steal. For where your treasure is, there your heart will be also."

This perspective shifts our focus from fleeting pleasures to enduring values, prompting us to invest in what truly matters: our relationship with God, loving others, and advancing His kingdom.

Strengthening Relationships

Believing in an everlasting God also impacts our relationships. It calls us to reflect God's unchanging love and faithfulness in our interactions with others. Ephesians 4:32 instructs us, "Be kind and compassionate to one another, forgiving each other, just as in Christ God forgave you."

Understanding that God's love is eternal encourages us to love others consistently and sacrificially. It also motivates us to seek reconciliation and extend forgiveness, mirroring the grace we have received from our everlasting God.

Facing Challenges with Confidence

Trusting in the power of the everlasting God equips us to face challenges with confidence. Knowing that God is with us and that His strength is limitless enables us to approach difficulties with faith and resilience. Philippians 4:13 declares, "I can do all this through him who gives me strength."

This confidence is not based on our abilities but on God's unchanging nature and His promise to be our ever-present help. Isaiah 41:10 offers encouragement: "So do not fear, for I am with you; do not be dismayed, for I am your

God. I will strengthen you and help you; I will uphold you with my righteous right hand."

Believing in the everlasting nature of God has profound implications for our lives. It means trusting in a God who is unchanging, reliable, and eternally present. This belief offers comfort and assurance, especially in times of uncertainty and difficulty. The power of the everlasting God can change our stories, offering hope, transformation, and salvation through Jesus Christ.

As we embrace the truth of God's everlasting nature, may we find strength and inspiration to live lives that reflect His unchanging love and faithfulness. In the words of Psalm 136:1, "Give thanks to the LORD, for he is good. His love endures forever." This declaration invites us to trust in the everlasting God, whose power and presence are eternal, transforming our lives with hope and assurance.

CHAPTER 07

THE THEOLOGICAL MEANING OF GOD AS EVERLASTING

The concept of God as everlasting is a cornerstone of Christian theology. This attribute of God implies His eternal existence, unchanging nature, and perpetual presence. Understanding what it means for God to be everlasting helps us comprehend His relationship with time, creation, and His people. This chapter explores the theological meaning of God as everlasting, drawing from scriptural references and theological insights to provide a comprehensive understanding of this profound attribute.

The Biblical Foundation of God's Everlasting Nature

The Bible frequently describes God as everlasting, emphasizing His existence beyond the confines of time and His immutable nature.

Old Testament References

One of the most explicit references to God's everlasting nature is found in Psalm 90:2, which states, "Before the mountains were born or you brought forth the whole world, from everlasting to everlasting you are God." This verse underscores the idea that God exists eternally, with no beginning or end.

Isaiah 40:28 also highlights God's everlasting nature: "Do you not know? Have you not heard? The LORD is the everlasting God, the Creator of the ends of the earth. He will not grow tired or weary, and his understanding no one can fathom." This passage connects God's eternal existence with His role as Creator, emphasizing His perpetual presence and unchanging strength.

New Testament References

The New Testament continues this theme, affirming the eternal nature of God. In Revelation 1:8, God declares, "I am the Alpha and the Omega," says the Lord God, "who is, and who was, and who is to come, the Almighty." This title indicates God's eternal presence, encompassing all of time from beginning to end.

John 1:1-2 speaks of Jesus, the Word, in eternal terms: "In the beginning was the Word, and the Word was with God, and the Word was God. He was with God in the beginning." This passage highlights the eternal existence of Jesus, affirming His divine nature and unity with the Father.

Theological Implications of God's Everlasting Nature

Understanding God as everlasting has significant theological implications. It shapes our understanding of His nature, His relationship with creation, and His interactions with humanity.

God's Immutability

One key implication of God's everlasting nature is His immutability, meaning He does not change. Malachi 3:6 states, "I the LORD do not change. So you, the descendants of Jacob, are not destroyed." God's unchanging nature is a source of stability and assurance for believers, as it means His character, promises, and purposes remain constant.

James 1:17 reinforces this idea: "Every good and perfect gift is from above, coming down from the Father of the heavenly lights, who does not change like shifting shadows." God's immutability ensures that He is always reliable and trustworthy.

God's Eternal Presence

God's everlasting nature also implies His eternal presence. Psalm 139:7-10 beautifully captures this truth: "Where can I go from your Spirit? Where can I flee from your presence? If I go up to the heavens, you are there; if I make my bed in the depths, you are there. If I rise on the wings of the dawn, if I settle on the far side of the sea, even there your hand will guide me, your right hand will hold me fast."

God's presence is not limited by time or space; He is always with His creation. This eternal presence is a source of comfort and guidance for believers, assuring them that God is always near, regardless of their circumstances.

God's Sovereignty and Eternal Plan

God's everlasting nature also underscores His sovereignty and the eternal nature of His plan. Ephesians 1:4-5 reveals that God's plan of salvation was established "before the creation of the world." This eternal perspective highlights God's sovereignty over time and His purposeful actions throughout history.

Romans 8:28-30 further emphasizes God's eternal plan: "And we know that in all things God works for the good of those who love him, who have been called according to his purpose. For those God foreknew he also predestined to be conformed to the image of his Son, that he might be the firstborn among many brothers and sisters. And those he predestined, he also called; those he called, he also justified; those he justified, he also glorified."

God's eternal plan encompasses the entirety of human history and extends into eternity, demonstrating His sovereign control and purposeful design.

The Everlasting God and Human Experience

Believing in an everlasting God has profound implications for how we live and perceive our existence. It influences our understanding of life, our response to challenges, and our hope for the future.

Eternal Perspective

Understanding God as everlasting encourages us to adopt an eternal perspective. This means recognizing that our lives are part of a larger, divine narrative that extends beyond our temporal existence. 2 Corinthians 4:17-18 encourages believers: "For our light and momentary troubles are achieving for us an eternal glory that far outweighs them all. So we fix our eyes not on what is seen, but on what is unseen, since what is seen is temporary, but what is unseen is eternal."

This perspective helps us prioritize what truly matters and invest in eternal values, such as our relationship with God, loving others, and advancing His kingdom.

Assurance and Hope

Believing in an everlasting God provides assurance and hope, especially in times of uncertainty and difficulty. Psalm 46:1-2 declares, "God is our refuge and strength, an ever-present help in trouble. Therefore we will not fear, though the earth give way and the mountains fall into the heart of the sea."

Trusting in the everlasting God means that we have a constant source of help and comfort, no matter what challenges we face. It assures us that God's promises are reliable and that His purposes will prevail.

Transformation and Renewal

The everlasting nature of God also brings hope for transformation and renewal. 2 Corinthians 5:17 proclaims, "Therefore, if anyone is in Christ, the new creation has come: The old has gone, the new is here!" God's eternal power and presence enable continual growth and renewal in the lives of believers.

Philippians 1:6 assures us, "being confident of this, that he who began a good work in you will carry it on to completion until the day of Christ Jesus." Our faith in the everlasting God gives us hope that we can experience continual transformation through His power.

Practical Implications of Believing in an Everlasting God

Believing in the everlasting nature of God has practical implications for how we live our daily lives. It influences our priorities, our relationships, and our approach to challenges.

Prioritizing Eternal Values

Understanding God's everlasting nature encourages us to prioritize eternal values over temporal concerns. Jesus teaches this in Matthew 6:19-21: "Do not store up for yourselves treasures on earth, where moths and vermin destroy, and where thieves break in and steal. But store up for yourselves treasures in heaven, where moths and vermin do not destroy, and where thieves do not break in and steal. For where your treasure is, there your heart will be also."

This perspective shifts our focus from fleeting pleasures to enduring values, prompting us to invest in what truly matters: our relationship with God, loving others, and advancing His kingdom.

Strengthening Relationships

Believing in an everlasting God also impacts our relationships. It calls us to reflect God's unchanging love and faithfulness in our interactions with others. Ephesians 4:32 instructs us, "Be kind and compassionate to one another, forgiving each other, just as in Christ God forgave you."

Understanding that God's love is eternal encourages us to love others consistently and sacrificially. It also motivates us to seek reconciliation and extend forgiveness, mirroring the grace we have received from our everlasting God.

Facing Challenges with Confidence

Trusting in the power of the everlasting God equips us to face challenges with confidence. Knowing that God is with us and that His strength is limitless enables us to approach difficulties with faith and resilience. Philippians 4:13 declares, "I can do all this through him who gives me strength."

This confidence is not based on our abilities but on God's unchanging nature and His promise to be our ever-present help. Isaiah 41:10 offers encouragement: "So do not fear, for I am with you; do not be dismayed, for I am your God. I will strengthen you and help you; I will uphold you with my righteous right hand."

The theological meaning of God as everlasting encompasses His eternal existence, unchanging nature, and perpetual presence. Understanding this attribute of God shapes our view of His character, His relationship with creation, and His interactions with humanity. It provides us with assurance, hope, and a perspective that transcends our temporal existence.

As we embrace the truth of God's everlasting nature, may we find strength and inspiration to live lives that reflect His unchanging love and faithfulness. In the words of Psalm 136:1, "Give thanks to the LORD, for he is good. His love endures forever." This declaration invites us to trust in the everlasting God, whose power and presence are eternal, transforming our lives with hope and assurance.

CHAPTER 08

THE PHILOSOPHICAL DIMENSIONS OF GOD AS INTRINSICALLY EVERLASTING

The concept of God as intrinsically everlasting transcends theological discourse, finding a significant place in the realm of philosophy. Philosophical inquiry into God's eternal nature seeks to understand how an everlasting being interacts with time, existence, and reality itself. This chapter explores the philosophical dimensions of God's intrinsic everlastingness, examining how this attribute intersects with concepts of time, change, existence, and metaphysics.

The Concept of Eternity in Philosophy

Eternity, in philosophical terms, refers to a state of being that is outside the confines of time. It is often contrasted with temporality, which is the state of being within time. Philosophers have long debated the nature of eternity and how it applies to the divine.

Timeless Eternity vs. Everlasting Duration

One significant philosophical distinction is between timeless eternity and everlasting duration.

- Timeless Eternity: This view posits that God exists outside of time altogether. In this conception, God does not experience temporal succession; past, present, and future are simultaneously present to Him. This perspective is often associated with classical theism and philosophers such as Augustine and Boethius.

- Everlasting Duration: This view suggests that God exists within an infinite duration of time, experiencing a sequence of temporal events. God has always existed and will always exist, but His existence is experienced as an unending sequence of moments. This perspective aligns with process theology and philosophers like Charles Hartshorne.

Both perspectives attempt to articulate how an everlasting God relates to time, each with its own philosophical implications and challenges.

God and the Nature of Time

Understanding God as intrinsically everlasting raises profound questions about the nature of time itself.

Philosophical inquiries into time often consider whether time is a created entity or a fundamental aspect of reality.

Time as a Created Entity

If time is a created entity, then God's existence precedes the creation of time. This aligns with the idea of timeless eternity, where God exists in an eternal present, independent of temporal constraints. This view suggests that time began with creation and that God, being outside time, initiated this temporal framework.

Time as a Fundamental Aspect of Reality

If time is a fundamental aspect of reality, then God's everlasting nature implies an infinite extension within this temporal framework. This view aligns more closely with everlasting duration, where God's existence stretches infinitely backward and forward within the realm of time.

Both views grapple with the nature of divine eternity and how it interacts with the created order. Philosophers such as Thomas Aquinas have argued for the compatibility of God's timelessness with His interaction in temporal events, suggesting that God's eternal nature encompasses all of time without being constrained by it.

Immutability and Change

Another critical philosophical dimension of God's everlasting nature is the interplay between immutability (unchangeability) and the capacity for change.

Immutability

The doctrine of immutability holds that God does not change. This attribute is intrinsically linked to His everlasting nature, suggesting that God's essence and attributes remain constant. Philosophers like Aristotle and Aquinas argue that because God is perfect, any change would imply imperfection, which is incompatible with the nature of a perfect being.

Capacity for Change

On the other hand, some philosophical perspectives, particularly within process theology, argue that God is dynamically involved with creation and therefore capable of experiencing change in relational aspects while maintaining His essential attributes unchanged. This view posits that while God's nature is immutable, His interactions with a changing world involve a form of responsive change.

This philosophical tension between immutability and change challenges our understanding of how an everlasting God can interact meaningfully with a temporal, mutable creation.

Existence and Ontology

Philosophical exploration of God's everlasting nature also delves into the ontology of divine existence—what it means for God to exist eternally.

Necessary vs. Contingent Existence

In philosophical terms, God's existence is often considered necessary, meaning that He cannot not exist. This contrasts with contingent beings, whose existence depends on external factors. God's necessary existence underlines His independence and self-sufficiency, reinforcing the idea that His everlasting nature is intrinsic and not dependent on anything outside Himself.

The Ontological Argument

The ontological argument, formulated by Anselm of Canterbury, posits that the very concept of God as the greatest conceivable being implies His necessary and everlasting existence. Anselm argues that if we can conceive of a being than which none greater can be conceived, this being must exist both in the mind and in reality, because existing in reality is greater than existing only in the mind. This argument underscores the philosophical claim that God's everlasting nature is a fundamental aspect of His being.

Metaphysical Implications

The metaphysical implications of God's everlasting nature extend to how we understand the structure of reality itself.

God as the Ground of Being

Philosophers like Paul Tillich describe God as the "Ground of Being," suggesting that God's everlasting nature is the foundation of all existence. In this view, everything that exists derives its being from God, who is the ultimate source and sustainer of all reality. This perspective reinforces the idea that God's eternal nature permeates all of existence, providing the basis for all that is.

Transcendence and Immanence

God's everlasting nature also speaks to the philosophical concepts of transcendence and immanence. As an everlasting being, God transcends time and space, existing beyond the physical universe. However, His eternal nature also means He is immanent, present within the creation, sustaining and interacting with it continuously. This duality highlights the complexity and depth of God's relationship with the world.

Ethical and Moral Dimensions

The philosophical exploration of God's everlasting nature also touches on ethical and moral dimensions.

Absolute Morality

If God is everlasting and unchanging, then His moral character is also absolute and unchanging. This provides a foundation for objective morality, suggesting that moral truths are grounded in the eternal nature of God. Philosophers and theologians argue that ethical norms and values are reflections of God's immutable character, providing a stable foundation for moral reasoning.

Human Response to the Everlasting God

Understanding God as everlasting also influences how humans perceive their moral responsibilities and ethical decisions. The awareness of an eternal, unchanging divine presence encourages a perspective that transcends temporal concerns, promoting values and actions that align with the eternal nature of God.

The philosophical dimensions of God's intrinsic everlastingness encompass a broad range of inquiries into time, existence, change, and morality. Understanding God as everlasting challenges and enriches our comprehension of reality, offering profound insights into the nature of divine eternity.

As we reflect on these philosophical explorations, we are invited to consider the depth and complexity of God's eternal nature. This reflection not only enhances our intellectual understanding but also deepens our appreciation of the mystery and majesty of the everlasting God, whose existence transcends time and encompasses all reality. Through this lens, we gain a richer, more nuanced perspective on the divine and its implications for our lives and the world.

CHAPTER 09

TIME AND THE DIVIN: EXPLORING THE RELATIONSHIP BETWEEN TIME AND GOD

Time is a fundamental aspect of human experience, shaping our understanding of existence, change, and continuity. The relationship between time and the divine, however, raises profound questions. Is time a creation? Is God outside time? When was the beginning of time? Can time be stopped? What is the relationship between time and humanity? This chapter delves into these questions, examining the nature of time and its theological implications.

Is Time a Creation?

The question of whether time is a creation is deeply philosophical and theological. The Bible suggests that time, like the physical universe, was created by God.

Biblical Perspective

Genesis 1:1 states, "In the beginning, God created the heavens and the earth." This verse implies a starting point not only for the physical universe but also for time itself. The "beginning" suggests the initiation of temporal existence.

John 1:1-3 echoes this idea: "In the beginning was the Word, and the Word was with God, and the Word was God. He was with God in the beginning. Through him all things were made; without him nothing was made that has been made." This passage reinforces the notion that all things, including time, were created through the Word, who is Jesus Christ.

Philosophical Perspective

Philosophically, time as a creation aligns with the concept that time is contingent upon the existence of the universe. If the universe has a beginning, then time itself must also have a starting point. This view is supported by many classical and contemporary philosophers who argue that time is not an independent entity but a dimension that began with the creation of the cosmos.

Is God Outside Time?

The idea that God exists outside of time is a central tenet in classical theism. This perspective asserts that God, being eternal and unchanging, is not subject to temporal constraints.

Timeless Eternity

Timeless eternity posits that God exists in an eternal present, where past, present, and future are simultaneously present to Him. This view is supported by passages such as Psalm 90:2, which states, "Before the mountains were born or you brought forth the whole world, from everlasting to everlasting you are God." Here, God's existence spans beyond temporal boundaries.

In Isaiah 46:9-10, God declares, "I am God, and there is no other; I am God, and there is none like me. I make known the end from the beginning, from ancient times, what is still to come." This suggests that God's knowledge and existence encompass all of time simultaneously.

Philosophical Implications

Philosophically, if God is the creator of time, He must exist outside of it. This aligns with the concept of God's transcendence, where God exists beyond the physical and temporal universe He created. Thomas Aquinas and other theologians argue that God's timelessness is essential for His immutability, as any involvement in time would imply change.

When Was the Beginning of Time?

Determining the exact beginning of time is a question that merges theological doctrine with scientific inquiry.

Biblical Account

According to the Bible, time began with the creation of the universe. Genesis 1:1-5 describes the first day of creation, marking the beginning of temporal existence. The phrase "In the beginning" signifies the commencement of time as part of God's creative act.

Scientific Perspective

From a scientific perspective, the beginning of time is often associated with the Big Bang theory, which posits that the universe began approximately 13.8 billion years ago. Before this event, the concept of time as we understand it did not exist. This scientific understanding can be seen as compatible with the theological view that time began with creation, though it frames the discussion within the context of physical cosmology.

Can Time Be Stopped?

The concept of stopping time is a common theme in science fiction but poses significant philosophical and scientific challenges.

Physical Impossibility

Scientifically, time is a continuous dimension that progresses irrespective of human perception. The laws of physics, as we understand them, do not allow for the cessation of time. Time is intertwined with space, forming the fabric of the universe, and cannot be halted without fundamentally altering the nature of existence.

Theological Reflection

Theologically, the idea of stopping time is not supported by scripture. However, the concept of eternity implies a state beyond temporal constraints. In the eschatological vision of Revelation, time as we experience it may be transcended, but it does not imply a cessation of existence or reality. Revelation 21:1-4 describes a new heaven and a new earth, where the former things have passed away, suggesting a transformation rather than a termination of time.

What is the Relationship Between Time and Humanity?

Time profoundly influences human existence, shaping our experiences, actions, and understanding of life.

Temporal Existence

Human beings are inherently temporal creatures. Our lives are marked by a beginning (birth), progression (life), and an end (death). Ecclesiastes 3:1-2 captures this reality: "There is a time for everything, and a season for every activity under the heavens: a time to be born and a time to die."

Human Perception of Time

Humans perceive time linearly, experiencing it as a sequence of events. This perception influences how we plan, remember, and anticipate. Time provides a structure for our existence, enabling growth, change, and development.

Theological Perspective on Human Temporality

Theologically, human temporality underscores the need for a relationship with the eternal God. Psalm 90:12 reflects this: "Teach us to number our days, that we may gain a heart of wisdom." Recognizing the finite nature of human life encourages a deeper reliance on God, who is eternal.

Redemption and Eternal Life

Christian theology teaches that through Jesus Christ, humans are offered eternal life, transcending temporal limitations. John 3:16 promises, "For God so loved the world that he gave his one and only Son, that whoever believes in him shall not perish but have eternal life." This relationship with the eternal God offers a future beyond the constraints of temporal existence, where believers partake in God's everlasting life.

The relationship between time and the divine raises profound questions that bridge theology, philosophy, and science. Understanding time as a creation aligns with the biblical account and suggests that God, as the creator, exists outside of time. The beginning of time is framed within the context of creation, both theologically and scientifically. While the concept of stopping time poses significant challenges, the relationship between time and humanity highlights the temporal nature of human existence and the hope of eternal life through Christ.

As we contemplate these dimensions, we are invited to appreciate the mystery and majesty of God's eternal nature. Reflecting on time and eternity deepens our understanding of our place in creation and our relationship with the everlasting God, whose presence and purpose transcend the temporal boundaries of our existence.

EMBRACING THE MYSTERIES OF THE DIVINE

The questions of God's existence, His name, and His authority are profound and complex, touching the very heart of our understanding of the divine. They invite us to explore the mysteries of the eternal, self-existent, and sovereign God, leading us into deeper theological reflection and spiritual contemplation. Throughout this exploration, we have sought to understand various aspects of God's nature, each revealing a glimpse into His infinite essence.

Understanding God's Existence

From the outset, the concept of God's existence challenges our finite minds. God is described as eternal, existing from everlasting to everlasting, with no beginning and no end. This eternal nature sets God apart from all created beings, emphasizing His uniqueness and self-sufficiency. The exploration of God's existence through scriptural references and philosophical reflection highlights the depth and mystery of the divine.

In understanding God's eternal nature, we recognize His unchanging character. Malachi 3:6 declares, "I the LORD do not change." This immutability offers comfort and assurance, knowing that God's promises and purposes remain constant throughout time.

The Name of God

The names of God revealed in scripture provide profound insights into His character and attributes. Names like Yahweh, Elohim, El Shaddai, and Adonai encapsulate different aspects of God's nature, from His self-existence and power to His lordship and sovereignty. Each name is not merely a label but a revelation of who God is.

Exodus 3:14, where God reveals Himself as "I AM WHO I AM," underscores the depth of His self-existence. This name signifies God's eternal presence and His unchanging nature. It reminds us that God is the ultimate reality, the foundation of all existence.

God's Authority

God's authority is intrinsic to His being, demonstrated in His governance of the world and His interactions with humanity. As the Creator of the heavens and the earth, God's authority is absolute and unchallenged. His sovereign will is reflected in the establishment of moral laws, the execution of justice, and the provision of salvation.

Understanding God's authority shapes our relationship with Him. It calls us to submit to His lordship and trust in His sovereign plan. Isaiah 46:9-10 reminds us of God's unparalleled authority: "I am God, and there is no other; I am God, and there is none like me. I make known the end from the beginning, from ancient times, what is still to come."

The Everlasting Nature of God

The concept of God as everlasting encompasses His eternal existence, unchanging nature, and perpetual presence. This attribute reassures us of God's reliability and faithfulness. Psalm 90:2 proclaims, "Before the mountains were born or you brought forth the whole world, from everlasting to everlasting you are God."

Believing in the everlasting nature of God has profound implications for our lives. It provides comfort and assurance in times of uncertainty, hope for transformation and renewal, and the promise of eternal life through Jesus Christ. Understanding God as everlasting encourages us to prioritize eternal values and live in alignment with His purposes.

Philosophical Dimensions

The philosophical exploration of God's everlasting nature delves into the nature of time, existence, and reality. The distinction between timeless eternity and everlasting duration highlights different perspectives on how God relates to time. Philosophers have debated whether God exists outside of time or within an infinite duration of time, each view offering unique insights into the divine nature.

Understanding time as a creation suggests that God, as the creator, exists beyond temporal constraints. This aligns with the theological perspective that God is sovereign over time, initiating and sustaining the temporal framework within which we live.

The Relationship Between Time and Humanity

Time profoundly influences human existence, shaping our experiences and understanding of life. Recognizing the temporal nature of our existence encourages us to seek a relationship with the eternal God. Psalm 90:12 advises, "Teach us to number our days, that we may gain a heart of wisdom."

Christian theology offers the hope of eternal life through Jesus Christ, transcending temporal limitations. John

3:16 promises, "For God so loved the world that he gave his one and only Son, that whoever believes in him shall not perish but have eternal life." This relationship with the eternal God transforms our perspective on life and eternity.

Embracing the Mystery

Throughout this exploration, we have encountered the profound mystery of God's nature. The finite human mind can only grasp so much of the infinite divine reality. Yet, this mystery invites us to a deeper relationship with God, where faith bridges the gap between understanding and belief.

Isaiah 55:8-9 captures the transcendence of God's ways: "For my thoughts are not your thoughts, neither are your ways my ways," declares the LORD. "As the heavens are higher than the earth, so are my ways higher than your ways and my thoughts than your thoughts."

Faith encourages us to trust in the revealed truths of scripture, even when they surpass our comprehension. Through faith, we can experience the transformative power of God's character, finding peace, purpose, and direction for our lives.

The exploration of God's existence, His name, and His authority invites us to delve into the mysteries of the divine and deepen our faith in the eternal, self-existent, and sovereign God. Through scripture, theological reflection, and spiritual contemplation, we gain a greater understanding of who God is and how He relates to His creation.

As we embrace these profound truths, may we be inspired to live lives that reflect the unchanging love and faithfulness of the everlasting God. In the words of Romans 11:33, "Oh, the depth of the riches of the wisdom and knowledge of God! How unsearchable his judgments, and his paths beyond tracing out!" This declaration reminds us of the vastness of God's wisdom and the beauty of exploring His divine nature.

APPENDICES

Appendix A: Key Biblical References on God's Eternal Nature

1. Psalm 90:2

- "Before the mountains were born or you brought forth the whole world, from everlasting to everlasting you are God."

2. Isaiah 40:28

- "Do you not know? Have you not heard? The LORD is the everlasting God, the Creator of the ends of the earth. He will not grow tired or weary, and his understanding no one can fathom."

3. Revelation 1:8

- "I am the Alpha and the Omega," says the Lord God, "who is, and who was, and who is to come, the Almighty."

4. John 1:1-2

- "In the beginning was the Word, and the Word was with God, and the Word was God. He was with God in the beginning."

5. Hebrews 13:8

- "Jesus Christ is the same yesterday and today and forever."

6. Malachi 3:6

- "I the LORD do not change. So you, the descendants of Jacob, are not destroyed."

7. James 1:17

- "Every good and perfect gift is from above, coming down from the Father of the heavenly lights, who does not change like shifting shadows."

8. Psalm 46:1-2

- "God is our refuge and strength, an ever-present help in trouble. Therefore we will not fear, though the earth give way and the mountains fall into the heart of the sea."

9. 2 Corinthians 4:17-18

- "For our light and momentary troubles are achieving for us an eternal glory that far outweighs them all. So we fix our eyes not on what is seen, but on what is unseen, since what is seen is temporary, but what is unseen is eternal."

10. John 3:16

- "For God so loved the world that he gave his one and only Son, that whoever believes in him shall not perish but have eternal life."

Appendix B: Philosophical Perspectives on Eternity

1. Timeless Eternity

- Concept: God exists outside of time, experiencing all moments simultaneously.

- Key Philosopher: Augustine, Boethius.

- Implications: Emphasizes God's immutability and omniscience.

2. Everlasting Duration

- Concept: God exists within an infinite duration of time, experiencing temporal succession.

- Key Philosopher: Charles Hartshorne.

- Implications: Suggests God's dynamic relationship with creation and capacity for relational change.

3. Necessary vs. Contingent Existence

- Necessary Existence: God must exist and cannot not exist.

- Contingent Existence: Created beings exist but are dependent on external factors.

- Ontological Argument: Posited by Anselm, suggesting that the concept of God implies His necessary and eternal existence.

Appendix C: Key Theological Terms

1. Aseity

   - Definition: God's self-existence and independence from anything else.

      - Biblical Reference: Exodus 3:14 - "I AM WHO I AM."

2. Immutability

   - Definition: The attribute of God that indicates He does not change.

      - Biblical Reference: Malachi 3:6 - "I the LORD do not change."

3. Omnipresence

   - Definition: The attribute of God that indicates He is present everywhere.

      - Biblical Reference: Psalm 139:7-10 - "Where can I go from your Spirit? Where can I flee from your presence?"

4. Sovereignty

   - Definition: God's supreme power and authority over all creation.

      - Biblical Reference: Isaiah 46:9-10 - "I am God, and there is no other; I am God, and there is none like me."

5. Eschatology

- Definition: The study of end times and final events in history from a theological perspective.

- Biblical Reference: Revelation 21:1-4 - The new heaven and new earth.

Appendix D: Practical Implications for Believers

1. Worship and Reverence

- Scripture: Psalm 145:3 - "Great is the LORD and most worthy of praise; his greatness no one can fathom."

- Application: Understanding God's infinite nature deepens worship and adoration.

2. Trust and Confidence

- Scripture: Isaiah 41:10 - "So do not fear, for I am with you; do not be dismayed, for I am your God. I will strengthen you and help you; I will uphold you with my righteous right hand."

- Application: Trusting in God's eternal and unchanging nature provides peace and stability.

3. Eternal Perspective

- Scripture: 2 Corinthians 4:17-18 - "For our light and momentary troubles are achieving for us an eternal glory that far outweighs them all."

- Application: Encourages believers to prioritize eternal values and invest in what truly matters.

4. Moral and Ethical Living

- Scripture: Ephesians 4:32 - "Be kind and compassionate to one another, forgiving each other, just as in Christ God forgave you."

- Application: Reflecting God's unchanging love and faithfulness in our interactions with others.

Appendix E: Reflections on Time and Eternity

1. Human Perception of Time

- Concept: Humans experience time linearly, as a sequence of events.

- Implications: This perception shapes how we plan, remember, and anticipate.

2. Divine Perspective on Time

- Concept: God's eternal nature encompasses all of time simultaneously.

- Implications: God's actions and plans are not constrained by temporal limitations.

3. Eternal Life and Salvation

- Scripture: John 3:16 - "For God so loved the world that he gave his one and only Son, that whoever believes in him shall not perish but have eternal life."

- Implications: Belief in Christ offers eternal life, transcending temporal existence.

These appendices provide additional context and insights into the profound themes explored in this book, offering readers a deeper understanding of the eternal, self-existent, and sovereign nature of God.

175

www.ingramcontent.com/pod-product-compliance
Lightning Source LLC
Chambersburg PA
CBHW051830150726
47998CB00001B/362